T0304935

SCREAMS

Also by Ysenda Maxtone Graham

The Church Hesitant: A Portrait of
the Church of England Today

The Real Mrs Miniver: Jan Struther's Story

Mr Tibbits's Catholic School

An Insomniac's Guide to the Small Hours

Terms & Conditions: Life in Girls'
Boarding-Schools 1939–1979

British Summer Time Begins: The School
Summer Holidays 1930–1980

Jobs for the Girls: How We Set Out
to Work in the Typewriter Age

SCREAMS

*Shrieks of Horror and Yelps of
Pleasure from Modern Life*

YSENDA MAXTONE GRAHAM

With drawings by Nick Newman

abacus
books

ABACUS

First published in Great Britain in 2024 by Abacus

3 5 7 9 10 8 6 4

A CIP catalogue record for this book
is available from the British Library.

ISBN 978-0-3491-4656-0

Typeset in Garamond by M Rules
Printed and bound in Great Britain by
Clays Ltd, Elcograf S.p.A.

Papers used by Abacus are from well-managed forests
and other responsible sources.

Abacus
An imprint of
Little, Brown Book Group
Carmelite House
50 Victoria Embankment
London EC4Y 0DZ

The authorised representative
in the EEA is
Hachette Ireland
8 Castlecourt Centre
Dublin 15, D15 XTP3, Ireland
(email: info@hbgi.ie)

An Hachette UK Company
www.hachette.co.uk

www.littlebrown.co.uk

January Screams

You start the year watching a revolting recipe

. . . being demonstrated on Instagram by a woman in gym clothes with long fingernails. Somehow, this social-media recipe-watching thing has become a time-consuming aspect of daily life, just because you once 'liked' someone's gratin dauphinoise.

It's horribly compelling.

The woman pours a colander of pre-cooked spaghetti into an ovenproof dish, then pours a jar of ready-made tomato sauce over it, then snips up a whole packet of sliced ham the colour of a dog's tongue and dots it all over, then empties an entire cylindrical pack of Boursin over it, plus some limp over-boiled broccoli (this must be happening in America; they do things differently there), then puts it all into her oven and takes it out a split second later, by which time it has turned into a 'cosy spaghetti bake'. She eats a forkful at her kitchen island, and does a little dance of joy.

3

You're watching this at the crack of dawn on New Year's Day. It can't be good for the gastric juices, to gaze at this kind of thing on an empty stomach.

'May I wish all my friends and followers a very happy and prosperous . . .'

Oh God, it's started: the liberal dispensing of 'Happy New Year' good wishes from famous thespians to their unfamous followers.

They expect you to lap up the goodwill with awe and gratitude, as if it were manna from heaven being generously sprinkled by the famous thespian over YOU. But that word 'all' makes it meaningless. It simply tells you that the actor has woken in a good mood and a benevolent frame of mind and has lots of followers.

No one wants to be classed as a member of a nameless crowd of millions called 'all'.

You feel bashed on the head and actually a bit bullied by this onslaught of blanket beneficence.

First cup of tea of the year, and the milk has gone off

. . . although the sell-by date is not till 5 January. This has happened because the milk carton is ridiculously enormous. They don't sell half-litre ones any more, let alone litre ones, in the nearby 'local' outlet of the supermarket chain, only two- or four-litre ones, designed for massive cornflake-eating teenaged rowers. You feel under constant pressure to make a white sauce to use up the stuff: a béchamel lifestyle you do not want to take up.

This vast carton has been weighing down the fridge door for over a week, putting a strain on the shelf, so you'll soon be squinting at the faded make and model number to recite it to the Beko small parts line. And now the milk plays its last mean trick on you.

You pour the required minuscule amount into the favoured mug with the favoured teabag in. Gasping with thirst, you pour in the kettle water. Hundreds of small white flecks rise to the surface with the urgency of champagne bubbles. The tea is ruined, the mug is sullied, the mug you have to use instead is not favoured, and the tea you have to drink is rust-brown and metallic-tasting.

On the hall shelf

... sits a shallow NHS cardboard box addressed to you, requiring you to send in a stool sample to check for bowel cancer.

You know deep down that this is not going to happen. The day will never come when you decide to tackle this particular mental block, requiring an unthinkable manoeuvre to do with spooning a sample into a test tube. How would you get purchase on it in the watery bowl?

But nor can you quite bring yourself to throw the box away, as this would be a wilful act of refusal to face God's truth. So there it sits.

You step out into the world, and a bright-green electric hire bike

... is lying in front of you on the pavement, casually discarded by its previous rider. It looks as lifeless as a dead cow. On its side, it takes up a vast amount of space. The carelessness of the person who finished his or her lazy, expensive, non-pedalling bike ride with this heartless gesture, and landed you with this unwanted item too close to your premises!

This is an example of 'Big Litter'.

A tiny, empty, fish-shaped plastic soy-sauce bottle from a box of sushi is lying in the gutter

So, someone affluent enough to buy a box of sushi, and greedy enough to consume it there and then, has been selfish and thoughtless enough to throw the miniature plastic bottle onto the pavement as soon as he or she has squirted out the last drop of soy sauce from it, perhaps annoyed that it ran out of soy sauce too soon, which it always does, as shops and takeaway cafés are so mean with their soy-sauce allocation.

You imagine the faint sucky noise the bottle made on its final squirt, and the frustration and disappointment of the sushi-eater who would now have to consume the final four rice-heavy items without the salty hit of soy sauce. Serves them right. What will future archaeologists make of the empty plastic fish?

This is an example of 'Small Litter', and it is as detestable as the fainted bike.

Vomit at the crossroads

This is 'Hogmanay' vomit. In its lumpy, semi-liquid way, it does actually look quite Scottish, like a spilled tin of Scotch broth.

It must be the calling card of one of the men who were hanging around in the middle of the night making loud grunts.

A scattering of raw onion slices

. . . are lying whitely on the pavement a few doors beyond, outside the kebab shop. These are not vomited onion slices, but discarded ones. Someone decided they didn't need quite so many onion slices on their kebab, which indeed they didn't.

A dog will eat those onions and will be poisoned by them, onions being one of the foodstuffs they mustn't eat, along with chocolate and raisins. The dog will then have diarrhoea.

So many stomach-churning food-related sightings in such close succession before 10 a.m. on New Year's Day: this will surely make it easier to start the January detox.

A stranger staring at her phone is walking straight towards you on the pavement

. . . not noticing you. She has earplugs in both ears, so she is not hearing you either. Basically, she's absent in every way except physically.

You decide to do something tinglingly enjoyable. You walk straight towards her, making a beeline for her body, just to see how long it will take for her to snap out of her phone reverie and notice you. Will she smash her forehead right into your face? She's about to. At the last moment she spots you out of the top of her phone-consumed eye, and looks up, annoyed (and a bit embarrassed?) that you're almost nose-to-nose and she hadn't seen you.

You experience the pleasing illusion of having 'taught her a lesson'.

Text arrives from friend, with five 'x's at the end

It's a 'Happy New Year' from one person especially to you! So it means something! Hooray!

But five 'x's? This x-flation is getting ridiculous. A couple of years ago, the convention was two. Then, all of a sudden, two seemed a bit formal and cold, so you both went up to three. Three meant 'very close friend indeed'.

Then this friend put her three 'x's up to four. So you had to do four back, so as to seem equally loving in return.

Thus the x-currency has inflated. You now need to keep a constant mental note of how many 'x's you give to each friend. There's the stern one-x-er, who sticks rigidly to one, refusing to play the escalation game. Good for her: an elegant move, although it can sometimes come across as a bit icy. Then there are the emotionally reserved perpetual two-x-ers; even two now look a bit unfriendly, as one 'x' used to. Then there are the reliable three-x-ers; that's the mass of close friends you'd invite to your birthday party. Then there are the unpredictable friends who vary from three to two to one, depending on the emotional heft of the message.

Now, in a sudden outpouring of love, your four-x-er friend has gone up to five. Five! How to respond? Has to be five back. Four would look as though you'd counted and thought five just one too many.

The panettone you were given for Christmas

... is still taking up space in the kitchen bread-bin, only a quarter eaten, still in its thick, loud cellophane wrapper. The stark fact is no one wants to eat it. The attractive tall, red cardboard packaging it came in – it did look splendid, an Italian marketing triumph, and how effusively you managed to thank the giver! – has long since been thrown away, along with the other festive wrapping, picked up by the bin men on their superb post-Christmas clear-up. So all you have left is this large lump of plastic-wrapped stale Italian cake, which isn't even quite cake, but a sort of sweaty cakey curranty bread, giving off the weird, sickly-sweet smell of a basement breakfast room in a family-run Italian hotel.

'I actually don't mind panettone, as long as it's toasted,' says the cheerful member of the family who claims to be willing to chomp his way through the stuff and insists, 'Don't throw it away.' But it's now five days into January, and he still hasn't got round to eating it.

You rashly went for the 'drop' Norway Spruce

... rather than the 'non-drop' Nordmann Fir, thinking it was the more elegant, discerning choice of pure-bred Christmas tree. But now the day has come for removing it, there's hardly any tree left.

It was already shedding badly by 19 Dec, and was pretty well bald by Boxing Day: just baubles on twigs.

But now, as you lug the poor thing out of the house, it does a final flourish, dropping its last few hundred needles onto the carpet and (somehow) into your underwear.

At least it's almost weightless as you carry it to the heap of dumped trees beside the recycling bins – the heap that started forming at teatime on Christmas Day with the first ruthless throw-out.

The New Year gym initiative

. . . is dampened by the fact that the thinner woman on the cross-trainer next to you is doing her exercise on a harder, hillier setting than you, and for three times as long. You glimpse across at her screen: '50 minutes remaining'. Fifty! So she's chosen to do this exhausting thing for a full hour, while texting. And she's clearly ten years older than you.

The undrinkable cappuccino in the café

It's freezing and you crave the comforting reward of a cup of coffee with foam on top.

In your imagination is the perfect cappuccino, the one you once had at a coffee house in Vienna, brought to you by a grey-haired waiter in black tie. It was small, exquisite, piping hot, its creamy foam marbled with a darker wisp from the rich coffee underlay. It was presented on an oval tray beside a glass of water with a spoon spanning from rim to rim, plus two sugar lumps and a Viennese biscuit. It was post-museum nectar for weary legs and Bruegel brain.

Here, you watch with mounting dismay as, for the second time this week, you encounter too much milk.

Why did you ask for a cappuccino rather than an Americano? It was because last time you ordered an Americano 'with hot milk on the side, please', the barista said, 'Oat milk?' and you replied, 'No, HOT milk', and she said, 'You mean oat milk?'

Today's barista, not barrister – you've heard that joke, and this one is more overworked than a barrister anyway – absorbed in milk-concentration, drips a tiny puddle of espresso into the bottom of a bowl-sized cup. She wipes the runny nose of the milk-frother, pours a massive amount of milk into a metal jug from a polythene carton inside a Tupperware box, froths it up, and then loads the cup with a baby's-diet amount of milk, before coaxing out lumps of foam to form a thick top layer.

It's the foam you've been fantasising about; the foam that will melt in the mouth, sweetened with the dusting of hot-chocolate powder.

As soon as you've had a few licks of that, you go right off the whole thing.

The bewildering choice of flushes

To get into the café's loo in the first place, you had to type in the code on the receipt: #3842. It's a roomy 'disabled' loo, all levers, ropes, panic buttons and bell-pulls.

And now there's a choice of flushes. Should you use the eco flush (the smaller chrome button on the right) or the fuller, more wasteful flush (the larger one on the left)? It's a borderline case. You press the eco-one and it doesn't quite do the trick. So you have to wait in the noxious cubicle for it to complete its pathetic throat-clearing little cycle and try again with the one on the left. And you have nothing to read except the words: 'Now wash your hands for twenty seconds'.

The confidence-sapping bike stand

Nipping out to do errands, you lock your bike to a bike stand which is wearing, around its ankles, two old D-locks that are still locked. They must once have been locked to bikes, but the bikes have gone. How did the person steal the bikes without unlocking the D-locks? It's a mystery, a conjuring trick known only by the Magic Circle of bike thieves.

Even if you're only rushing into the shop for five minutes, those minutes are now fraught with anxiety. Right now, out there, somebody might well be enacting the 'separate bike from locked D-lock' trick, and when you come back, your bike will be gone. You'll report the crime to the police, who will close the case within twenty-four hours.

Daffodils before snowdrops

Something has gone very wrong with the natural order of flower-appearance. February used to be the month for daffodils to start being sold too early in British supermarkets. But now they appear in January, before the snowdrops in the garden have come out.

These daffodils must have been specially propagated and force-grown in a micro-climate across the Channel before travelling to Britain in a refrigerated lorry.

They've gone up from the previous £1 a bunch, so this is no longer Daffodil Poundland, but £1.50 is still far cheaper than the usual price of bought flowers.

The poor things are lying bone-dry in a green plastic basket beside the till, so the only kind response is to snap up seven bunches and fill every room with them. They look beautiful.

God, this music is so sad, it's worming its way into your soul

This is the music the customer helpline plays while you are waiting to get through to a human being.

You can't avoid listening to the music they play to you. It's like waiting for a bus: you can't read, as you need to be on constant lookout for the arriving bus. While kept on hold, you can't concentrate on anything else, as you need to be in a state of hyper-alertness, just in case the repeated 'We are experiencing an unusually high volume of calls; please continue to hold and your call will be answered as soon as possible' ever gets converted to a 'Hello, I'm an actual human being, how may I help you?'

What they really mean is: 'It's not cost-effective for us to employ enough people to answer the telephone.'

This department's music is particularly wistful: a repeated guitar piece with a deeply melancholic strain. They keep you on hold for an hour and a quarter. Fifteen minutes in, you start to cry, because the music, which you've now heard repeated multiple times, is so sad, with its lurch into a minor key halfway through each rendition, and because your country is so broken if it makes you listen to this for an hour and a quarter when you need to talk to a human being.

A human being used to be called 'a person'. But now you have to call them 'a human being', actually naming the species, because talking to one is so rare and needs to be distinguished from answering questions to a pre-recorded voice which says, 'I'm sorry, I didn't quite hear that'.

'You've come through to the wrong department. You need to hang up and dial again, pressing option four'

'No! No! Please! Please, please don't go! Please don't leave me! I've been waiting an hour and a quarter to get through. I pressed all the options the voice told me to press. Please don't make me hang up. Can't you just put me straight through to the person I need to talk to? Please? What's your name?'

You think that if the human being gives you his name, you might be able to strike up a friendly, constructive relationship, and also, you'll be able to report him if he's really unhelpful.

'It's Barry'

. . . he ventures, and it's in a friendly Irish accent. He's melted! You have tapped in to his humanity with your own pleading and sweetness and your own humanity! You've smashed through the wall of automation and bureaucracy! Joy and relief spread through your body. You still live in a country where, if you do eventually get hold of a human being, even if he's in a call centre on the other side of the globe,

or just in County Cork, you can work your magic on him, and breathe warmth into him, and almost make friends.

And he does help! He looks up your files and genuinely does 'get back to you', after a much briefer second spell on hold, and the impossible thing you're caught up in does get a tiny bit more sorted.

For the rest of the day you'll bang on about 'My new best friend, Barry' who was 'so helpful and kind'.

You're still in a state of rapture when you receive the email asking for feedback. 'On a scale of 1 to 10, how satisfied were you with the service?' '10!' 'On a scale of 1 to 10, how likely would you be to recommend us to someone else?' '10!' In a few words, please can you explain why you were satisfied?' 'Because Barry sorted my problem.' Lovely, lovely Barry.

Throwing an iron away

You have to, because it suddenly stops working, in the middle of ironing a shirt, a few weeks after its one-year warranty period is up. You try changing the fuse and of course that doesn't work. So, it's over.

You can't be expected to book a trip to the dump just to get rid of an iron, can you? (And you do have to book a trip to the dump these days, and you have to prove you're a local resident. They've made it so you can't just turn up, on a whim, with an iron.)

So, to get rid of the thing, you stash it in the kitchen

bin, hoping no one will notice, but it's heavy and still hot. The pointy end melts a hole in the bin liner, and you know the bin men will see what you've been up to and will probably reject the bag and label it with a 'naughty' sticker which everyone in the street will see.

You can't recycle the lids of the tinned tomatoes

. . . only the tins themselves, according to the strict crosses and ticks on the recycling sack. So there's nothing for it: at some point, while making the Bolognese sauce (the planned detox is not happening; life is much too busy for self-indulgent fasting), you'll need to do the final pulling off of the lids of all three tins of tomatoes, with index finger through the ring-pulls. 'Let's pull the whole thing off.'

This final pulling off of the lids produces splashes of red juice over your clothes, your face and the wall.

'Have we watched this episode?'

. . . of the *Line of Duty* spin-off? It's 'Series 3, Episode 4'. You can't remember. The snapshot of the episode on the streaming homepage – two characters in police uniform talking to each other beside a police car – doesn't look particularly familiar. So perhaps you haven't watched it?

But you have a feeling you did watch Episode 4 of Series 3. For some reason, it's not showing the blue line of watchedness, or saying 'resume'. So you're confused. The only thing to do is fast-forward to the middle of the episode and take a sample.

You forward the cursor and stop it at a random moment, and the same two people in police uniform are talking to each other beside a police car. Maybe you have seen it? Or was this another programme you fell asleep while watching?

February Screams

Nespresso-machine absent-mindedness

Did you or did you not put the capsule into the machine? This is the kind of habitual daily gesture it's terribly easy to lose all recollection of doing or not doing.

The closed capsule-holder isn't giving a thing away. So the choice is: to open the capsule holder to check whether you did put one in, which risks the wasting of 45p, because if you did, the opening of the capsule-holder will cause the capsule to fall straight into the machine's mini-bin (but if you forgot to put one in, you'll be vindicated); or to press the 'make cup of coffee' button and risk watching a 'lungo' amount of revolting pale brown water dripping down, and you can't stop it, as that would confuse the machine, so you have to stand there watching it do its long-drawn-out programmed action in full.

'Oxfordshire village road closed for resurfacing works'

Are you really such a dull person that, when you go into Google first thing in the morning, this is the top article from today's national journalism that comes up, tailor-made to your specific interests? It's true, you did once travel to Oxfordshire and you did check the status of the roads before the journey and you did get quite interested in one particular road closure. But that was a year or so ago.

The awful thing is, you now can't resist clicking on the headline. 'Drivers are being told to "seek an alternative route" when travelling on the A4130 through Brightwell-cum-Sotwell.' This is strangely compelling to read about, as enjoyable as hearing about a tailback on a far-away motorway on the Radio 2 travel bulletin. You're almost tempted to drive to the vicinity of Brightwell-cum-Sotwell to see the fun with your own eyes.

And because you clicked to have a look, you come across as someone definitely interested in this facet of life, and will now get alerts about new traffic lights in Chipping Norton.

'Some personal news to share'

So posts a woman you've never heard of, thrilled to announce she's been promoted to a job title you've never heard of at an organisation you've never heard of.

'PIN OK'

That's so reassuring to see! They told you it didn't work when you just tapped your card onto the machine. So you were worried your bank account had been stripped out, or that you had been de-banked or somehow didn't exist. But the machine now recognises and accepts your PIN number! 'Pinok,' you whisper to yourself, saying it as one word, as it looks: like the harpsichordist Trevor Pinnock. You are verified.

No thank you, you don't want to give them your 'reasons' for unsubscribing

You just want them to leave you alone, for ever. Don't call me, I'll call you.

Having clicked on 'unsubscribe' and seen the announcement that 'you are now permanently unsubscribed', the very next thing that happens, two seconds later, is: you get an email from them saying, 'It won't be the same without you.' Eff off.

Parking in a rectangular parking space in a multi-storey car park designed before the invention of the rhomboid parking space

Rhomboid spaces are infinitely better. Can't the car-park-designing world realise that? You can just sidle into them with one deft right-turn of the steering wheel. (But are rhomboid spaces less efficient than rectangular ones, space-wise? You'd need to ask your old maths teacher, who may well still be alive.)

You know from experience that you must do all you can to avoid parking in a non-rhomboid rectangular slot which has a car on one side of it and a concrete pillar on the other, risking a catastrophic plummeting in value of the car as it scrapes along one or the other. It's worth going up or down to the next floor in the low-ceilinged hellhole of the car park to seek a better option: a free space next to another free space. But there isn't one. The only free spaces are the ten empty disabled spaces. And there's now a car behind you who'll grab the single space if you don't.

How to do this? You know you'll need to reverse into the space. You remember from bitter experience that trying to go forward into it will get you no more than halfway in. So you go beyond the space, with the indicator on, making it clear to the car behind, by panic-telepathy, what you're intending to do. The act of trying to reverse brings you out in a sweat: BO in both armpits. All music in the car must be switched off, for total concentration, like the lights dimming in a landing plane. The beeps of the sensor speed up. You're about to bump into the other car, or the pillar, or both.

No – it's impossible. Can't be done. You lose all desire to go shopping and realise you can live a full enough life without washing pods, Marmite and kitchen rolls.

The knickers on Instagram

They're beautiful. Not remotely thong-like, none of the up-the-crevice weirdness. They're brushed-cottony, bikini-style, purple and deep pink with creamy lacy edges, and perfectly, snugly fitting.

Then you realise: it's not the pants you crave. It's the model's buttocks. Don't be fooled.

But maybe your buttocks will magically become like the model's, if you put those pants on. Not an ounce of fat on them, just a few goose pimples on the bronzed and tanned glutes.

So you click on 'shop now' but resist the temptation, not sure which size you are. Now, every day for the rest of your life, those knickers and those perfect buttocks will appear before you.

'Just confirming that your phone number is 077 . . .'

And the person on the phone starts reading your own mobile phone number back to you, to check it's right, but they read it in the 'wrong' batches of numbers, not at all as you think of it. The double numbers are separated. The batch of digits you think of as a cosy five-some is split apart, so you hardly recognise it and can't say whether they've got the number right. It all sounds so strange and alien.

Yoghurt pots no longer have snap-on transparent lids

. . . which is good for the planet, but you now have to peel off the stick-on plastic lid and, instead of throwing it away as you used to, keep it and hope the adhesive quality of the yoghurt itself will act as the 'glue' to hold it on for the rest of its time in use.

'My writing room in the morning'

So posts the famous author (. . . and by the way, here's a glimpse of my Georgian old rectory, and no, I'm not telling you precisely where it is, because that would invite burglars, but just look at my writing room! Look at those open sash windows and the carpet of crocuses as far as the eye can see beyond that oak tree. You can see from this snapshot alone that my house is worth well over £4 million, and that's because I had the foresight to marry a hedge-fund manager.)

'OK, bye'

. . . you say at the end of the call to the technician. And the man who's been helping you doesn't just say 'bye' back. He says, 'OK, bye, bye, b-b-b-bye, bye.' It sounds like Morse code. It's not a stammer. It's an affectation. It makes him sound busy, hurried and a bit Australian, as he goes on to his next call.

'Have you got a moment to complete our customer survey?'

. . . asks the shop you frequently use. It's a 'Have Your Say' initiative.

Well, OK, if they insist, but please make it snappy.

It turns out not to be the work of 'a moment' at all. You're expected to position your feelings on their strange ladder of degrees of agreement, when they ask you to gauge your response to statements like 'I can nearly always find what I'm looking for'.

'Strongly agree.' 'Agree.' 'Not sure.' 'Disagree.' 'Strongly disagree.' None of these quite does justice to your precise level of assent or lack of it.

Avocado disappointment

If only one of the statements had been: 'Our "perfectly ripe avocados" are always perfectly ripe.' No doubt about the appropriate response to that. 'Strongly disagree.' The ripeness is always either recently passed or yet to come.

You pierce today's 'perfectly ripe avocado' with the sharpest knife (the one that says 'ice-hardened' on the blade, not the old one that says 'Sainsbury's', which you can't get rid of, as knives, like irons, are tricky to throw away).

No way will this February avocado be an easy-slicer, an easy-stoner or an easy-peeler. It's a sawing job just to cut it in half, and when you try to prise it open with the 'pushing cupped hands in opposite directions' action, a wodge of avocado comes off with one of the halves, stuck to the stone. You need a knife to peel the whole thing, as if it were a Granny Smith apple. Then you have to slice the stuck stuff off the stone, encountering the stiff resistance that tells you you're going to have indigestion all afternoon.

'Look at this photo of us all in Yorkshire!'

... says the friend, who then scrolls through her photos and can't find the one she's looking for. 'I know it's here somewhere. No it's not that one, it was before that ... Oh yes and here's one of Olivia at that amazing New Year's Eve party she went to in Sussex – look, that's her, and that's her lovely boyfriend, they're so sweet together, aren't they, but where's the one I wanted to show you?'

Her head is bowed, and she's absorbed in her extensive photo collection, and you just sit there waiting for as long as it takes.

Misericord seats on station platforms

Too high up for anyone under five foot five, and not proper seats at all, just orange plastic oblongs at a raked angle to lean your bottom against, new railway station 'seats' are exactly like the misericords medieval monks were obliged to lean back on during the interminable divine office, only far uglier.

Why the minimalism, and why the seat-meanness? Why can't you be allowed to sit down properly on an actual bench, on this draughty, comfortless railway plat-form where your train is 'expected' seven minutes late, at 17:51, and that has just gone up to 17:56? The long, leaning wait is minor torture, the 'expected' arrival time nudging forward minute by minute, always just out of reach.

There's plenty of room for proper benches. But platform-furniture designers clearly think it's slovenly to sit down. They probably designed those leaning seats from their own standing desks, feeling smugly dynamic about how standing up all day energises you. It doesn't. It tires you out.

'We apologise for any inconvenience this may have caused'

... says the announcement, when the 'expected time' has nudged forward to twenty minutes late.

Any inconvenience? *May* have caused?

Surely, that should be 'THE inconvenience this HAS caused'. That 'any' is a slippery way of making light of THE damage and boredom this lateness HAS inflicted on your day and your life.

Curvy sliding lavatory doors in trains

Why do they need to be great curvy, sliding doors? Why not just a flat door, that you open, close and lock, as is normal for loo doors all over the world?

But no. It has to be curvy and automatic. So, going to

the loo on a train becomes a theatrical performance in which you are the solo actor. Everyone near you watches as you enter and then stand there with your back to them while the door rotates very slowly behind you. The fact that the 'lock' sign is on the far side of the room, away from the door, makes you worry it won't work – which makes for a nervous, inhibited pee.

And will it open again? Or will you be locked into this spacious, circular disinfectant-scented sci-fi prison, where the flush is hidden behind the seat lid so you have to touch the lid and smash it loudly down, making your audience think of you as a seat-smasher?

Of the soap, water, hand-dryer trio

. . . in the train lavatory, one of the three doesn't work. The permutations are: soap and hand-dryer but no water (so you emerge with sticky, soap-smelling hands); water and hand-dryer but no soap (so you emerge still fundamentally unclean); or water and soap but no hand-dryer (so you emerge wiping your wet hands on your dry-clean-only trousers). Today's is 'no soap'.

Ready to face your audience, you stand facing the curvy door as it slowly opens, and you reappear, visibly relieved if not completely clean.

There's a long stretch of silence and nothing happening

. . . when the train stops at the station and you press the 'open' button but the doors won't open. You press it again. They're still not opening. You start to panic that the train will pull away, never having bothered to open its doors.

It's bad enough for the people on the platform, needing to get on, who'll have a long wait for the next train, but it's worse for you, trying to get off. You have the added layer of claustrophobic 'Get me out of here!' angst, desperate to escape from the hermetically sealed interior. On both sides of the door, frantic button-pushing is going on, until, the eventual 'beep-beep-beep' and the gassy noise of opening doors.

The slowness is all to do with health and safety, but don't they care about claustrophobia and panic?

Just because your beloved aged relative's charging hole has stopped charging

. . . she is told that she'll need to buy a whole replacement 'tablet' – the charging hole is unmendable, apparently. (And yes, of course you've tried 'cleaning it out', first with a toothpick and then with a paperclip, as demonstrated on YouTube, and neither of them worked.)

So you grab a new one for her, because she'll pay

anything, anything to have a working 'device'. Her whole quality of life depends on it.

This leads to a full day down the rabbit hole of password hell, hunched over her screen and your and her phones and her old paper lists of scribbled-down passwords from the last decade, trying to 'get back in' to every single thing she relies on, from shopping to radio-listening to reading to banking, and it's no fun at all to be asked the security question (middle name of her spouse), (a) because the spouse has died, which is unbearably sad, and (b) because the bank doesn't even recognise his middle name as the correct answer, so you try again, thinking perhaps it was the other spouse who first registered, so the middle name they might need is hers, but she has two middle names, and neither of them works, and the app now tells you you've 'tried too many times', and locks you both out.

You set the walking and cycling app

... to 'record', as you set out for the afternoon walk you haven't done before. But a mile into the walk, you make a mistake, walking the wrong way along an Aldi car park, before realising that the turn-off to the footpath is actually round the corner just before the store.

If you click on 'save activity', which you'll need to do in order to gaze at your walk statistics, that mistake will be preserved for ever more, and the three people who follow you on the app – and occasionally give you 'kudos' for your achievements – will see the embarrassing doubling up of the orange line, signalling your failure to read a map properly and to spot helpful signs and arrows.

And you haven't even got anything you're watching to look forward to for the evening

... because you still haven't found the right series to follow the one you watched that was life-changingly good and that you still think about every day.

You're lost when you haven't got anything good to watch. It's a real marriage-dampener.

So desperate are you to find something good for the evening that during the daytime, you secretly stump up £79.99 for an annual subscription to a new streaming channel in order to try out a series Mark Kermode said was 'completely immersive' and brilliant. It turns out to be an incomprehensible, confrontational, exhausting mess.

The next day, you pay for Series 1 of something from the 1990s that you've never got round to watching, that Clive James raved about in his book about box sets. But it's all fuck this, fuck that, fuck the fucking motherfucker in the drugs world, and you can't work out what's going on and nor do you care.

And the next day a friend tells you to 'persevere with it'. No thanks.

But then you tell your friends to 'persevere with'

... the brilliant series you recommended to them, the one you can't stop thinking about, which they claim to be 'not really enjoying' and they 'can't get into', although they've 'tried the first two episodes'. What's wrong with them? You thought they were kindred spirits, but they're clearly not. What a disappointment.

March Screams

*'Specialist subject - my computer
password security questions.'*

Stillborn tulips

The daffodils have vanished from the shelves, ridiculously early, because everything ends too early these days, and it's just tulips now – much more expensive, and (distressingly) often stillborn.

They look attractive in their cellophane packets in the shop, but after you've plonked them up to their necks in a vase, they lose even the semblance of retaining the will to pretend to live. Unable to take in water, they never progress from bud to bloom, but just freeze, in exactly that same state, hanging their heads and dying in bud. What evil was done to them in their stripy Dutch mega-field?

Stillborn light bulbs

Next, you climb up the stepladder to try to install a new downlight to bring a patch of light to the corner of the bathroom where darkness has fallen. The light bulb turns out to be stillborn too. It's brand new, but it doesn't work. You hold it to your ear and shake it, and it makes a pathetic little rattle denoting 'dead'.

Well done, car! You know it's raining

So clever of you! Yes, there are a few drops of rain! You noticed! And you've brilliantly instructed your wipers to do three or four slow sweeps.

What a delight the auto windscreen wiper is! Occasionally the car doesn't quite cotton on to the changeable weather, and fails to react, or sometimes it overreacts and starts madly wiping on the 'frantic' setting at the first soupçon of a raindrop, but you forgive it, because it's only trying to look after you and genuinely seems to have your best interests at heart.

'It's [your beloved friend]'s birthday today. Please help them to celebrate'

... says your Facebook 'feed', as always hedging its bets and avoiding the issue of the precise sex and gender of the friend whose birthday it is.

The terrible thing is, though, that the Facebook friend (woman) has died. In fact, she died five years ago, and no one has told Facebook. It makes you really sad to see her sweet face gazing out at you on what would have been her birthday.

'A password must be entered for this data transfer'

... say the words on the black screen in your car, when all you're trying to do is listen to a podcast on Bluetooth, and your phone is suddenly 'not recognised'.

The screen has never said those words before. What do they mean? Does the car really think you speak its incomprehensible language and are impressed by its use of the passive voice? The only reaction you're offered, in response to this chilling announcement, is to press the button which will say 'OK'.

But this is not OK.

So you listen to the podcast on your bed instead, in the late afternoon

. . . and it sends you into a deep sleep. Falling asleep to the sound of a podcast is one of the delights of modern life. Podcast presenters and their interviewed guests should not think of their soporific effect as a failure. It's a sign of success. In order to fall asleep to a podcast, it needs to be a really good one, so that you're briefly captivated by precisely how, for example, plankton came into existence in the oceans three billion years ago, and the next thing you know, you wake up forty-five minutes later in the middle of a completely different episode, and the one you were listening to says 'recently played'.

OK, so the heat pump will have to go there, will it?

In the useful place outside the back door where you now keep the outdoor freezer and the onions? A vast white metal item costing £30,000 with a fan making a terrible hum all day and night, and not heating the house, because these things don't work, but they're going to ban gas boilers, so you'll be forced to seal up your windows and live in an airless but still chilly house and won't be allowed to complain.

'I can never log in to anything, ever!'

. . . says the other, less-computer-savvy person in your life. It does indeed seem like a jinx. Every time he tries to log in to one of the few websites into which he has once logged, it doesn't work. 'So click on "forgotten password?",' you gently advise. So he does. He enters a new password but it says he can't use it, as he has already used it, so the new one has to begin with the number 11 and have a 'special character' at the end, and he will forget this one too.

Hamlet is a 'special character'. So is Macbeth. An exclamation mark does not feel like a special character.

'What was the name of your first school?'

Now, that is a nice security question! It's the one you need to answer in order to access your bank's tech helpline. How sweet of them to ask such a question about your childhood. You eagerly type in the name of your first school, quite hard to spell, and are transported back to the cine-camera days of early childhood: grazing your knee on the tarmac of the playground and throwing the lukewarm contents of the third-of-a-pint bottle of milk into the flower bed before going back into the classroom for a bout of reciting the three-times-table in unison.

But then it asks

... 'what's the name of your favourite sports team?'

Did you really once accept that as one of your three chosen security questions? You don't even have a favourite sports team. You can't think what you might have said. You try the son's favourite football team, but it spits that out in red lettering: 'Answer does not match'.

So, you now have to identify which of nine squares has a photo of a bridge in it, and some of the images are a little bit bridge-like but perhaps not quite bridges, and they're asking you to tick bridges at a stressful moment like this? Then you have to re-enter a new security question, and they're all stupid because they're not factual questions and you would answer them differently on different days. 'What was your favourite children's book?', 'What's your favourite colour?' Which imbecile designs these questions?

Landline rings at lunchtime

You know it's going to be the weekday lunchtime cold-caller, callously trained to call the fragile, gullible wife or widow at home on her own.

But you feel you must answer it, just in case it's someone telling you that a close family member has died. It could definitely also be that. Flooded with dread that it is indeed that, you pick up the phone.

Silence. Click. Call-centre background din. 'Am I speaking to . . .?' And then they get your name a bit wrong.

The only thing to do is to put the receiver straight back down. You know it's not the caller's fault. He's only doing his job. And, poor thing, his calls are 'recorded and monitored for training purposes', which is the way they bully them. But you mustn't get into conversation with him, or you'll be coaxed into signing up to something.

No hello, no goodbye. This is alienation at lunchtime.

'The middle act drags'

So writes the film critic, of the new film tipped to win nine Oscars, directed by the famous director now in his eighties.

Of course the middle act drags. The critic was clearly bored stiff. The film is three hours and twenty-five minutes long, for goodness' sake.

Nothing will entice you to go and see this masterpiece. By 'the middle act', the critic is referring to the middle two hours, when you would be stranded in mid-ocean, far out of sight of the shore of the beginning, and far from the shore of the end: the promised land of the rolling credits and the imminent glass of wine.

The self-indulgence of these directors, who allow their films to be this bloated! How can they expect anyone to go in to a cinema at teatime and emerge into the darkness of mid-evening, sadder and wiser after watching their slow, wistful, upsetting historic scenes?

The only good thing about the middle act is that, during it, you can sneak out to the lavatory and enjoy five minutes in this world, looking at your phone. How you've missed it! Being stuck in a long film at the cinema makes you homesick for this world, even if it's only the 'lavatory cubicle and quick look at social media' aspect of this world.

It's Saturday afternoon, and you hear an eruption of joy

... coming from the men watching football in the next room, when a goal has been scored. Huge release of pent-up energy and emotion: a 'scoregasm', as Jilly Cooper calls it. Then, a strange muffled silence. Then, quieter voices and a down-turning at the end of each muttering. It can only mean one thing. VAR must have disallowed the goal.

Too much truth doesn't make for happiness.

'He's picked up the ball at the halfway line

... and he's hit it ...' says the commentator. He's speaking in the 'sport tense', a football-commenting tense all of its *own, part of the comforting background noise of Saturday afternoons.*

If it were you describing what just happened on the pitch, you'd say, 'He picked up the ball at the halfway line and he hit it.' That's the normal past tense, describing something that just happened. But these pundits speak in the present perfect, which makes it all sound more immediate, especially when spoken in urgent Estuary followed up by agreeing Glaswegian.

'Last collection: 9 a.m.'

... says the red pillar box into which you've just posted the thank-you letter at 10 a.m. This beginning-of-day timing for postal collections is out of sync with the way most people live. So, your letter will sit in the bottom of this pillar box for another twenty-three hours, and the friends you've at last got around to thanking will have to wait till at least the day after tomorrow to realise that you are, in fact, a polite and grateful person who does write thank-you letters.

The man walking his dog has AirPods in both ears

... which look a bit like hearing aids, but they're not, although he may well need hearing aids soon if he continues to pour decibels into his waxy earholes all day.

He's clearly lost in his own audio world. Doesn't even notice you. So does that mean it's not worth trying to say hello to him or ask him how old his dog is? It does. He won't hear you.

Hinge of laptop goes weak

... like the cheaply made hinges of a 1970s Green Shield Stamps leatherette folding alarm clock, so the laptop flops open far too wide, and stops working, the vital connection between screen and keyboard broken.

It suddenly seems extremely odd that the old-fashioned invention, the hinge, devised by the Ancient Egyptians, should be such an intrinsic component of the computer age. Of course the hinge is going to go weak. Of course someone's going to open the laptop too wide by mistake, after which it'll never be the same again.

Either businesses don't take cash or they only take cash

... it's rarely a bit of both any more, and in the case of the hand-car-wash (badly needed after the filthy, muddy, weirdly dusty winter), they only take cash. And you haven't got any. So you have to walk a third of a mile round the one-way system to find the nearest cashpoint, sweating with worry about being hated, because there are three unwashed cars queueing behind you, the closest one a BMW which looks particularly mean and impatient.

The butternut squash you've lugged home

... to make a nice 'soup for springtime' is as hard and heavy as a rock. And it has no flat edges for any kind of stability. How are you meant to make any headway into it with the knife? It's all very well hoping to make the mouth-watering butternut squash and pancetta pasta dish you've found on the internet, but all you can see in your mind's eye as you stand poised (once again) with the sharp knife is the four-and-a-half-hour wait in the Accident and Emergency queue with nothing to read, while you slowly bleed to death.

There's nothing for it but to go into the vegetable at its waistline, sawing gently backwards and forwards, turning it slowly round, remembering to try to preserve your own life at all costs.

You could have bought the packet of ready-cut-up butternut squash, but that always smells faintly sweet, stale and already rotting.

Amazing! You've managed to cut the whole thing in half! But now what? Try to peel it? No peeler is sturdy enough for its ultra-tough hide.

Half an hour later, exhausted, but still alive, you have

in front of you a mountain of yellow cubes: far too much for the recipe.

A person you follow has been to a ceramics exhibition in Stoke-on-Trent

... and has posted a 'story', with twelve little white dashes along the top, each one denoting a photograph of a ceramic that you're now going to have to look at. You've been meaning to go to this exhibition but know you'll never get there. So you start looking at the photos. The first one is of a bowl. It takes a long time for the dash to chart its agonisingly slow course from left to right, meaning 'beginning of looking at this photograph' to 'almost time for the next photograph'.

At last, it leaps over the gap to the beginning of the next dash, but – the anticlimax! – it's the same bowl. The photo hasn't changed. This accidental repetition in her line-up of photographs diminishes your appetite for the bowls, for the exhibition and for Stoke-on-Trent itself.

OK, so the dark blue dots

... on the West End theatre's seating plan mean 'tickets available at £255 each'. They're at the front of the Dress Circle, exactly where you'd like to sit, and exactly where you used to sit when taken to the theatre as a child. But now far too expensive.

The dark purple dots, hardly distinguishable from the dark blue ones, mean 'available at £190 each'. There are two dark purple dots left, towards the back of the Dress Circle. So, you'd still be paying loads and wouldn't be able to see very well.

What about the dark red dots? Ah, that means 'available at £120 each', and there are four left in the back row of the stalls, which would be that dark place under the roof of the Dress Circle which always feels as if it's about to drop onto your head. No good, and still extortionate. Ah, the yellow dots mean 'restricted view' and are £55 each. That's more like it. So even if you hate the play you won't both hate it and feel ripped off. But you'll definitely hate it if you can only see half the stage.

Driving through an unknown British town in the dark, looking for somewhere to eat

... you see a sign which you think says 'trattoria' but on closer inspection says 'tattoo parlour'. Then you see a sign which you think says 'bar' but on closer inspection says 'nail bar'.

The high street is deserted. Is there anywhere to eat in this down-at-heel market town which gets an enthusiastic mention in Pevsner but has clearly fallen on hard times?

You order a bowl of pasta each

... for £12.99 a portion, at the Italian restaurant you do eventually find, plus a glass of house red each, and two espressos. So how on earth does the bill come to £66?

The pasta's not nearly as good as the pasta dishes you make at home on a daily basis.

The car's satnav can't cope when you stop for petrol on the motorway on the way home

It might be clever in other ways, but in this regard, it's thick. 'Recalculating', 'rerouting', getting into a panic, saying 'proceed to route shown', when you're simply trying to do the very thing it needs in order to get anywhere in the first place.

In a way it's endearingly psychologically rigid and un-adaptable. But come on. Calm down. Get the hang of it. You're only going to a petrol station, not a scrapyard.

Then, to mock the satnav even more, you decide to take another route home from the one it recommends

... and it absolutely hates that.

Baiting the satnav is a joy of modern life.

You know your chosen route is actually faster, or at least certainly no slower, than the satnav's suggested one. But it goes into stubborn, bossy, know-all mode, instantly punishing you by downgrading your expected arrival time to fifteen minutes later.

'Take the next exit,' it commands; in other words, 'Do a U-turn at the roundabout, and don't you dare try to outwit me again.' You see the proposed U-turn on the diagram – the blue line going up towards the circle and then turning back on itself and coming down again.

No! You're not going to take that exit.

At first, as you're driving under the bridge which you would have driven over if you'd taken the exit, the satnav thinks you have obeyed it. 'At the roundabout, take the fourth exit,' it commands.

But then it realises you've gone past. It must recalculate.

'In two miles, take the exit . . .'

Nope!

How long will it take it to get what you've decided to do? How long till it bends to your will?

It's a blissful moment when, at last, it gets the point and meekly agrees to go along with your plan.

Then it has to go through the ultimate humiliation of admitting that the expected arrival time is actually the same as its original estimation. Ha ha!

On arrival home, you feel compelled to make soup

... out of the remaining batch of butternut squash cubes, in order not to waste them.

You can no longer just bung an onion and a potato into a pan to make soup 1980s-style. You now have to do the whole trendy 'soffritto' thing of frying finely chopped celery, carrot and onions for ages on a low heat, to 'make the base'. That's what modern soup expects of you.

The chopping! The effort! The time it takes! The danger to the fingers (again, especially with carrots, which are rock-solid in the centre, like the core of the earth). All for a soup that won't even count as 'something to give the family for supper', because it won't be filling enough.

Then, in a state of absent-mindedness, you lift the Braun hand-blender out of the thick orange liquid a split second before releasing your thumb, so it spurts round the room in a mini-tornado.

'Wait for it'

... says the Instagram reel, in which a dog and a child are about to do something funny, sweet and hilarious, but they want you to watch the build-up to the funny, sweet, hilarious moment.

Yes, that's the truth about contemporary humanity's

pathetically short attention span. We wouldn't bother to wait for it if they didn't say 'wait for it'.

Now it's you listening to music as you walk the dog on the fresh spring morning

... and when it's you doing it, not someone else, it's not annoying, but ecstatic. One of the great classics of the European romantic repertoire is blaring into both your ears, a heroic backdrop to your humdrum life. Wet grass, fallen twigs, litter bins, grey sky – and the opening movement of a sublime masterpiece.

In order not to be annoying like everyone else is when they wear headphones on walks, you make a special effort to smile at passers-by, to show them you're not just any old headphone wearer, but a really nice one, present in this place and available to be said hello to and smiled at. Strangers probably think you're a bit creepy when you smile at them inanely in this way, clearly experiencing some kind of aural epiphany.

April Screams

'The Lord is risen. He is risen indeed.'

'Hallelujah.'

It's Easter morning.

But what happened to the spontaneity?

It's all written down on the service sheet: the vicar must announce that the Lord is risen. And that he is risen indeed. That second sentence adds as much as 'and a merry old soul was he' does to 'Old King Cole was a merry old soul'.

You then have to respond with the assenting 'Hallelujah', as if in raptures. It's like being in a studio audience when you're told to clap or laugh. It comes out sounding wet and downbeat.

Nearly time to sing the first hymn

... but the modern hymn books are too large to fit onto the narrow ledge of the Victorian pew in front of you: a ledge designed for the pocket-sized *Book of Common Prayer* in the era of tiny fonts and India paper.

Nervously, you lay the hymn book down, and it sticks out far over the edge of the shelf. As with a balanced see-saw, one tiny touch, or even just a blow of your breath, will bring the whole book crashing to the floor.

You try opening it to the correct page for the first hymn on the hymn board and propping it up against the pew, in its open state, but this is just as precarious, as the ledge is polished and slippery and the book won't stay open.

It's as tricky as trying to lay out a picnic on a fold-down train table.

This might be the last line of the sermon

It's been going on for quite long enough.

'... and this, my friends, this is what God calls on us to do, not just on Easter Sunday, not even on every Sunday, but on every day of the week, and, yes, every day of the year.'

But, dismayingly, it isn't the last line. It was a false ending. He takes a deep breath and carries on. He's like the dinner guest who gets up to leave but is still chatting in the hall half an hour later.

The collection purse is passed along the pew

... and you have to pass it on to the next person with an embarrassed smile, because you forgot to bring any cash. The next person does exactly the same. Poor church, literally.

A new BBC television true-crime documentary series starts on Easter Monday

... and it opens with an introduction that lasts for five whole minutes, set to thundering piano music, in which the entire series is laid out before you in taster form. Snatches of interviews: a woman saying 'we had no inkling', and a man saying 'I can honestly say it was psychologically devastating'. On it goes, still to the pum-melling background music, the narrator now saying, 'This story will take us from the shores of west Ireland, to the streets of Brussels, to a small village in Sweden. It's a story of greed, of longing, of chinks of light in the midst of darkness, and of one man's quest to discover the truth.' Still not finished. Another interviewee says, in Swedish, with subtitles, 'He seemed such a friendly guy – we really liked him at first', and a disturbed-looking young adult says, 'This village has seen a lot in its history, but never anything like this'. Then a clergyman says, 'Only God knows what goes on deep inside the hearts of men.' And, as the music crescendos, the narrator says, 'What unfolded over those months reveals facets of human nature that, once seen, can't be unseen.'

Only then, at last, does the actual first episode begin. You know it has started, because the music has changed to cheerful baroque, to denote 'beginning of actual episode' and 'what seemed like an ordinary weekday morning in a bustling market town'.

Did you need that long-drawn-out introduction to cajole and hook you into watching the series? You did not. The 'taster' was too much like the whole meal. You're sort of sick of it all before it even begins.

'How come we're still subscribing to this streaming channel?'

Because you never stopped. Even though you haven't watched anything on this channel for months. And unless and until you do stop, you'll be living in the servitude of automatic renewal. They know they've got you for life, unless you can be bothered to go to 'manage accounts' and 'remember password' and be asked to fill in a sad questionnaire about why you're leaving.

You scan your club card at the supermarket

... but the price doesn't go down. Not even by a penny. That's horrid. What's the point of a club card if the price refuses to budge? And in what way can this be described as a 'club' anyway? Are they laying up some kind of treat for you in the future, such as an eventual 2-for-1 voucher on your favourite Lurpak, perhaps in two months' time? Is that their idea of something to look forward to?

'Except cycles'

Cul-de-sac sign, no entry sign, car and motorbike inside red circle sign, 'No through route', 'Controlled Zone', planters, bollards, camera, 'At any time' sign, speed bumps, double red lines, no left turn, no right turn, Ultra Low Emissions sign.
    But it's OK! Because today you actually ARE on a bicycle! For once, this sign-heavy new world is designed especially for you. You breeze through the Great Barrier of Negativity, while everyone around you is stuck in a traffic jam.

'You have now reached your limit of three free articles a month'

... says the magazine's website.
    How mean of them. Probably mean of you, actually,

rather than of them, but still. You desperately want to read this one. But you're not going to subscribe. You already subscribe to seven other things plus (it now seems) five streaming channels. It's mad. You'll have to read it in a magazine aisle, trying not to be noticed as a non-paying content-guzzler.

'I'm sorry but we're no longer allowed to help you fill in the form'

. . . says the bank clerk in the local branch, which is struggling on, but has the sad atmosphere of a bank branch soon to be closed down.

They've tried to make bank-going more like going to chat to someone in their home, removing the forbidding glass-fronted counters and just having nice 'greeters' in the bank's livery standing behind small high tables, but this change actually has the effect of making you know for certain that they won't be able to help you with the particular knotty problem you're encountering.

They're no longer allowed to help you to open a new bank account. This must be a time- and labour-saving directive. All they're allowed to do is to sit and watch while you try to do it yourself. So you feel like you're a child at a Montessori school where the teachers have been trained to 'watch the children learn things for themselves' rather than actually teach them.

Trying to text the word 'its' and autocorrect changes it to 'it's'

'There's a special place in Hull reserved for the inventor of autocorrect,' you mutter to yourself, still finding that quip quite funny, years after you first heard it.

OK, no ticket office any more

... so you go to the ticket machine, and jab at the alphabet letters to 'select destination' so hard with your index finger that it hurts. The machine doesn't respond to the letter-jabbing. The kind, patiently impatient man behind you shows you that you need to jab a bit higher up, just above the letters. That works better, and it's actually nice seeing, as you get closer to typing the full name of the destination, the choice of possible next letters diminishing and the suggestions of which station you're trying to go to coming up.

But are you allowed to select a Super Off-Peak day return, seeing as you might well be coming back again during what could be classed as some kind of rush hour? There's no one to tell you.

'If you see something that doesn't look right . . .'

You just have. It's a pug: a dog designed not to be able to breathe properly.

But they don't mean that.

'. . . speak to one of our operators, or text the British Transport Police on 61016. We'll sort it.'

Come on. Spit it out. Here it comes.

'See it, say it, sorted.'

You've heard it spoken in so many different recorded voices – men, women, northern, southern, cockney, posh, lisping – and they all do it a bit differently. It's as if they're being auditioned for RADA or LAMDA. Today's nicely spoken voice, a woman's one, puts special emphasis on 'say it' with an upward but non-questioning inflection at the end, as if to suggest that it might suddenly occur to you to 'say it', and that this would be an inspired and supremely intelligent idea.

Has anyone ever seen it and said it, and was it sorted?

'. . . or text the British Transport Police on 61016.'

Oh my God! This is an actual human being speaking, right now, into a microphone on this very train, and he's rebelling.

He's not going to follow those words up with the required mantra. He stops right there, letting the imagined words hang unspoken in the air.

It's a huge relief. As with the relief when a car alarm cuts off in the middle of the night, the silence is a physical pleasure.

'Have you got the tickets?'

'Yes, they're on my phone' is the smug answer to that question. Of course you've got the tickets, and they're e-ones. Gone are the days when you were expected to 'print tickets at home' and arrive clutching a folded sheet of A4.

But when you try to show those tickets to the sweet out-of-work actor on the door of the theatre, you can't find them anywhere in your phone's email inbox. You try tapping in the name of the theatre, but nothing comes up. 'Who should the email be from?' you ask the person on the door, who surely must know the answer because lots of people must surely ask it. But he doesn't. You try 'noreply@', 'boxoffice@', 'info@' and 'orders@' but it's nowhere to be found. In a state of sweaty anxiety, you eventually type in the name of the play. That triggers something deep in the phone's memory, and at last the tickets appear. The confirmation email turns out to be from 'rachel@'. How could anyone be expected to guess that?

The plastic tumbler for the G & T you're allowed to bring into the auditorium

... is so thin and soft that even just holding it, as lightly and delicately as you can, causes you to squeeze the tumbler so the drink spills out from the top.

And everyone else laughs

... at a line you don't find funny. The loneliness of that! Straight-faced and unamused in a world of guffawing.

Then you have to walk past three urinals

... in order to reach to the unisex loo in the interval.

To non-urinal users, urinals are strangely shocking to look at, because they are so clearly designed specifically for one thing only: pee-aiming from the penis. Bidets are also quite shocking to look at, being designed purely for French people to wash their bottoms after sex. To look at a bidet is to think of that and that alone. But urinals are worse, because they also emit a strong smell: an overpowering mixture of male urine and disinfectant 'urinal cakes' that hang around near the plug hole.

The oval shape of a urinal resembles the open-mouthed 'oh' of shock on encountering one.

Everyone around you stands up during the final applause

... and you feel like a churlish misery-guts as you sit there, stony-faced, politely clapping but refusing to join in with the standing ovation, and now you can't see a thing because there's a row of other people's backs and bottoms in front of you.

May Screams

It's the No-Mow season. The grass in the park is ankle-deep

This prolongs the life of the insects that will feed the birds and caterpillars, but around you, park-goers are dealing with the side-effects. One woman is rubbing her shoe backwards and forwards, having trodden in a dog's mess hidden deep in the meadow-like fronds. Another is searching in vain for the poo that her own dog looked as if it was doing. Children and dogs are rummaging for lost balls. The whole place looks chaotic: an unweeded garden that goes to seed while the mowers are sitting idle for a month.

But it's fun watching the British Military Fitness people

... toiling away on the unmown grass, being bellowed at by a sergeant-major-type trainer, encountering God knows what beneath their press-ups. You check your watch and see it's only ten past something, so they've got at least twenty minutes of the torture still to go, if not fifty.

They look the opposite of attractive with the huge numbers on their backs, which they like because it makes them feel impersonal, military and cathartically bullied.

'Get on court'

... says the sign on the fence of the municipal tennis courts, encouraging the whole community to keep fit. That sounds hideously coarse, compared with the more gentle 'Anyone for tennis?'

The sterile front garden

No soil, no trees, no plants, no weeds, no flowers, nothing alive at all: just white stone paving. All perfectly neat, but dead and totally inhospitable to any passing worm or snail. Can't the tidy, bookless bores who designed their beige interiors and their white-stone front garden see that they're doing their bit to shut off the possibility of life to small animals desperately in need of somewhere to live in this increasingly paved-over postcode?

No, please don't tell me every single thing you had to eat

... on the 'tasting menu' at the Michelin-starred restaurant you went to last night. That'll mean having to be interested in seven courses, or was it nine?

'So, first they brought us this tiny brioche with I think it was rillettes, and a sort of fig jam, and then it was two unbelievably delicious scallops with tiny circles of black pudding, and I think it was a sort of pea compote, an amazing kind of pale green foam, really, and then we had a tiny glass of elderflower sorbet, you wouldn't think you'd want it but it was actually perfect, and then they brought us these thin slices of fillet steak, with truffle purée ...' And you find yourself counting and thinking, 'How many more to go?'

And then they say, 'And amazingly, I didn't come out feeling too full up. These menus are really well designed so you don't feel bloated.'

(And now please don't name the different wines they brought you with every course.)

Sweet Instagram video of a Labrador

. . . gently lifting a kitten in its mouth, by the scuff of its neck, to make it take part in the photo shoot on the doorstep. Next, there's an American baby breaking out into a beaming smile when his 'Mom' puts a pair of spectacles on him for the first time and he can see the world. You know it's a displacement activity to scroll through this stuff, wasting months of your life, but it actually makes you cry, and millions of others must be doing it too as this one has had 2,986,254 likes.

The new tower block

You didn't ask for it; you wrote a letter to object to the building of it, but no one took any notice. And sure enough, three years later, here it is, blocking the sky, completely out of scale with the neighbourhood, red lights winking at night at the top of its surrounding cranes, as they stand by to finish the job of building thirty-two floors of unaffordable housing.

Dead box trees and dead box hedges

. . . everywhere you go, stripped naked by the invasion of the Asian caterpillar. So it's just pale-brown skeletons of box trees and box hedges now. Hard to imagine those days when you planted a green box hedge and it stayed as a green box hedge.

The pine cone on the antique chair

... in the drawing room of the National Trust stately home on the first May bank holiday is supposed to be a tactful and eco-friendly way of implying 'please refrain from sitting down on this chair' without having to write those words on a notice. It's passive-aggressive. Just looking at the pine cone sitting there infuriatingly right in the middle of the cushion of the Hepplewhite chair makes your legs ache and brings on a yearning to collapse into that very seat. Would you even bother to remove the pine cone? Probably not. You'd sink down and feel it just between the buttocks. Anything, anything to be allowed to sit down.

'Software update tonight'

So your phone informs you, out of the blue. You feel it's saying it in a breathy whisper. My goodness, you might not have any plans for tonight – just an evening in, drifting off to sleep with the telly on – but your phone is getting excited. 'Software update tonight,' it keeps whispering, whenever you look at it after ten minutes of not looking at it.

For the phone, tonight is a sexy date.

But the next morning

... the phone informs you that (very sadly) it was 'unable to install update' as 'some apps weren't responding'.

This feels depressingly like the message you get the morning after meeting a stranger through online dating: the anticlimactic 'I'm afraid it didn't really work for me and I didn't feel the chemistry was really there' message.

The phone says it will 'try again tonight', but it doesn't sound quite as excited the second time round. Its fear of dysfunction is now palpable.

'No, you do NOT need to translate that bit of French for me'

... you hiss at the book you're reading, whose author and/ or publishers clearly think you're so badly educated that you need to have the words *'après moi, le déluge'* translated into English in brackets straight after they appear, or, worse, at the bottom of the page as a footnote. So patronising! You went to school, for God's sake.

Bad radio moment

... when, driving the car and desperate for something good to listen to, every radio channel fails you at the same time.

On Radio 4, the scientist you've never heard of is telling Jim Al-Khalili about the lab he worked in for three years before he was promoted to a more prestigious lab.

On Radio 3, they're playing a glass-shattering Italian aria over-sung by a famous diva from the past.

On Radio 2, they're playing a love song from 1974 so cheesy that it makes you feel sick.

On Radio 5 Live, they're speculating on next week's by-election results.

On Classic FM, they're playing the theme of a film you loathed, the one with the grand piano on the beach, and then telling you to relax.

On Absolute, it's the ad break.

At this moment, when the airwaves are crackling with dross, you fear for civilisation.

'Spaffed up the wall'

... is a revolting expression, making one think of a man masturbating and ejaculating while standing up, half-dressed, probably in the office. And of the result of this against the paintwork.

And yet politicians use this hideously coarse expression, in public, when referring to money wasted by someone else.

'I was fascinated to discover that I'm actually 3 per cent Munster Irish'

... says the friend who was given a DNA testing kit for his birthday and waited for the results to come back, which they just have. You feign interest but, really, this is not information of any interest to anyone except the 3 per cent Munster Irish person.

Is a double question mark a bit aggressive??

Yes, it certainly is. Look at it. It comes at you with its jerky, question-question hook-shape up against your face. You feel compelled to act on it instantly, and to agree or consent to whatever the sender is asking you to agree with or consent to. It's coercion dressed up as a question.

Then Facebook informs you that one of your friends is now following you

... which is lovely! One more for the tally. And there's a message from this new Friend. It says, 'Hi there.'

Then, a few hours later, 'How are you doing?'

Then, the next morning, '??'

But you know that this friend would never say 'How are you doing?' That sounds too American for him. He just might type 'How are you?' but even that would be a bit dull for him. And, an eloquent and good-mannered person, he would never, ever follow up an unanswered question with a double question mark and no words.

Facebook Messenger did it. It decided it needed to kick off the conversation between you and your new Friend by putting that snatch of stock international small talk into his mouth.

Will your old phone cover fit onto your new phone?

No. It's half a centimetre too small.

Does the shop where you're buying the new phone stock a cover that will fit the new phone?

No. They don't sell accessories.

Is the shop across the road which used to sell phone accessories still going?

No. It has closed down.

Can you live a relaxed life without a phone cover?

No.

Walking to a new destination with Google Maps directing you

... you can't work out whether you're going in the exactly the right direction or exactly the wrong one. It doesn't help that the voice says 'head north along the A501', because you have no idea which road that is or which direction north is.

It's confusing, because it's hard to remember whether the pale blue triangular fan-shape coming out from the blue circle which represents 'you, walking' is supposed to be coming out of the back of you or the front of you.

In any cartoon of someone walking or running, a ripple is shown to be coming out of the back of the person, designating the displacement of air in their wake.

But it turns out (after you've walked for seventy seconds in the wrong direction) that in Google Maps, the fan-shape actually comes out of the front of the walking person, from the tummy, as it were, or like a Dalek holding its arms forwards as it walks.

'Swim anticlockwise'

. . . says the sign at the deep end of the indoor pool. It also says 'Slow Lane', because this is the lane you've chosen to swim up and down twenty times.

There's only one other person swimming in the slow lane: a very old lady wearing a pink bathing cap who's swimming incredibly slowly on her back, using a pink foam 'noodle' to rest on. Somehow she and the noodle keep getting in your way. She's not obeying the 'swim anticlockwise' rule but is floating at a snail's pace right down the middle.

'This pool ain't big enough for the both of us,' you find yourself muttering in an American accent, like a cowboy in a Western who's finding it impossible to coexist in a one-horse town with a gun-toting villain.

Perhaps you should have plumped for the 'fast lane'. But that's a terrifying environment, currently occupied by three splashing men doing the crawl, one of whom is wearing flippers. If you tried to hold your own in the fast lane, swimming at your normal respectable speed, you'd be the annoying person to those Mark Spitz-types, and that would be even more psychologically exhausting.

You definitely did type the same four digits in to the changing-room locker

… after the swim as you did before it. The four-digit telephone number from childhood, the one that means so much.

But the locker doesn't recognise the code. A repelling red light flashes when you're expecting the green flash of unlocking.

So, dripping wet, shivering and towelless, you have to pad off to the reception desk and plead. The kind woman, looking weary from having done this too many times, accompanies you back to the changing room, and you have to speak to her in your most well-spoken voice so she trusts you not to be a thief, as she unlocks the locker with her skeleton code.

Swimming-pool lockers are a good reason not to go swimming.

LED light bulbs

. . . simply don't 'go'. It's extraordinary. After all those painful craning years at the top of the stepladder, when as soon as one bulb was replaced, another went and you had to get the stepladder out again, an electrician suggests you 'change to LED'. And you find yourself living in a new paradise of seemingly eternal light. The electrician tells you that you won't need to buy any spares, 'because these ones last fifty thousand hours'.

Fifty thousand hours? So if you have the kitchen lights on for, say, five hours per day, that means these ones will last for twenty-seven years? So by the time you do have to get the stepladder out again, you'll be too old to climb it.

The disappointment of the takeaway

Surely they used to be delicious, and generous?

As with the cappuccino, you have in your mind the memory of the perfect takeaway you once had on returning from a northern holiday on a rainy night in about 2003. There was a real sense of plenty: copious onion bhajis, creamy korma, fluffy rice and the unbelievably good minty yoghurt. And it cost £26.

Now the same thing costs £82 and the korma is nearly all liquid, with just three or four bits of chicken floating in it, as mean as prisoner-of-war soup, and from the meat's scragginess you somehow know this was a chicken, or a crowd of chickens, who lived a miserable life.

And rather than being delivered by someone who works at the actual restaurant, of the same nationality as the cuisine, it's delivered by an exploited delivery company driver with no personal connection to the restaurant, who's being sent round the city at 20 mph by faceless in-structions on his phone, feeding the greedy and the lazy. You feel sullied to be encouraging this gig economy that's making the wrong people rich.

And they forgot to include the poppadoms.

Season 3 of the series you've been addicted to

... is turning out not to be as good as Season 2, which itself was not quite as brilliant as Season 1. Quality is turning into quantity.

This is especially dispiriting if the character you loved best was killed off at the end of Season 2. You now have to start all over again in a state of bewildered grief, trying to drum up interest in someone new.

It's not nice to feel an addiction waning.

June Screams

Wedding invitation arrives

… and it's worryingly thick – as thick as the kind of envelope you get when you've been accepted rather than rejected by a school, university or firm. It turns out to be a kind of welcome pack, with the first names of the bride and groom in italics on the front, containing eight separate information cards, stipulating everything from 'gifts' to 'local hotels and hairdressers' to 'dress code'.

One of the information cards, the most ominous of all, spells out the full timetable for the wedding. Absent are the reassuringly simple words 'and afterwards at the Old Rectory': those wonderfully open-ended words, with no time stipulations. You could just slip away from that 'and afterwards at' kind of wedding.

Not from this one. Your presence is required by the bride and groom from 4 p.m. on Friday afternoon for an 'Edwardian tea', till 3 a.m. on Sunday morning, when the whole thing will eventually wind up, under the named activity of 'carriages'.

The wedding day itself, Saturday, requires you to turn up at the venue at 11.15 a.m., forty-five minutes before the 'ceremony', and then, after the 'photographs', to make your way to the reception venue, a hotel, where you'll be served 'champagne and canapés' for a full three hours before the sit-down 'wedding breakfast' which starts at the non-mealtime of 5 p.m. and goes on for another two and a half hours.

The cutting of the cake will then take place at 7.30 p.m., and the speeches from 8 till 9, followed by 'dancing', and 'bar will be open'.

You'll hardly be able to stand up by the time the longed-for 'carriages' moment arrives.

This is the bride and groom's vision for a thirty-five-hour adulation marathon from their friends, who must jump to their every requirement to prove their love.

Today's American home cook with varnished nails on social media

... is emptying a box of dry rice into a baking dish, then pouring two cans of Campbell's condensed chicken soup over it, then filling one of the cans with water and pouring that over it, then opening a sachet of 'ranch dressing' powder and scattering that over it, then draping six floppy chicken breasts over the whole thing and putting it all in the oven covered with foil, then taking it out and showing us the beige result, and then saying, 'My family loved it and asked for more'.

Shamefully, you find your mouth watering: salivation at the thought of the monosodium glutamate in the ranch dressing.

No, you've just BOUGHT a swimming costume online

... so please don't keep showing photos of swimming costumes for sale. Halter-strap costumes, long-body costumes, high-waisted bikinis, 'tummy-control casual one-piecers' ... a curated collection especially for you, swimming costumes popping up at all four corners of the screen all day long. The whole point is that you've just bought one, so you no longer need one. How do you get that message across to them?

But a delicious feeling of smugness and well-being

... fills your heart when you're sitting in an English garden on the day when all British airports grind to a halt during the summer half-term holiday due to an IT malfunction. Oh my God, you've GOT to watch the Six O'Clock News, to see

those poor people standing in an endless switchback queue at Heathrow, scrolling their phones in frustration and desperation, and a man fast asleep on the floor of the departure lounge with his suitcase as pillow, and a whole blonde family in shorts in Majorca who now can't get home as all the aeroplanes are in the wrong places and the chaos will continue 'until Sunday at the earliest', and they've been told to 'find a hotel', but there aren't any, and all the airline staff have vanished, and there's no one to help them and no one cares.

You did the right thing! You stayed at home in your safe, predictable little world.

'Strictly no cash on this ride'

The funfair has come to the green, Kidz World, and the whole postcode of young families is now being ripped off by it. 'Strictly wristbands only, or pay by card at kiosk, £1.20 per ride or £10 for 10 rides.'

But no one wants ten rides on the little cars that go round and round for two minutes at today's health-and-safety speed.

'That reminds me: what is for tea?'

That's the dachshund talking, in the sponsor's advertisement for Vitality Insurance, before and after each segment of the cricket match on Sky. Sometimes the dachshund says, 'Outings – better than innings.' It's not funny the first time and is repeated at regular intervals throughout the five-day match.

The whole world is not nearly as interested in the Glastonbury Festival

... as you are, middle-aged columnist in your high-end yurt.

The wooden spear plunged through the middle of the hamburger

... poses a challenge to the pub-garden hamburger eater. The many-layered hamburger was described on the blackboard as a 'short rib and flank burger, smoked Applewood cheddar, burnt onions, gherkins, skin-on fries', the vocabulary designed to justify the price of £17.50. The wooden spear (made of a thin shard of bamboo) looks quite pretty, with its curly knotted top that your fingers itch to unravel. But the spike gets in the way, in the way that a closed umbrella on an umbrella stand does when it's permanently plonked through the central hole of a garden table, so you can't see the people sitting opposite.

Yes, the spike does do the job of holding the hamburger

together – it would surely splurge apart with great uncontrolled oozings if it didn't have this dagger through its bleeding middle. But in order to eat it, you have to chomp your way slowly round and towards the spike, risking endless pokes in the eye, never sure when it's safe to take the spike out before tackling the final central mouthfuls.

'A607 closed after Syston'

... says the sign on the A road you're driving on, and you don't care. Because you're not even planning to go on the A607, and have no intention of going to Syston, let alone beyond it. So this closure is actually bliss to contemplate, being someone else's annoyance and not yours.

As is 'Queue after Jct'

... when you're planning to leave at jct. Let others have a terrible time, in the world beyond the jct, while you dart off onto the slip road into freedom. Today is your lucky day.

The level-crossing barriers

... stay down for too long: three whole minutes.

It's exciting at first, because if you've either ever been

a child or had a child, you never quite lose the thrill of 'guessing which direction the train's going to come from'. The tension mounts as you wait for the always-astonishing sight of an actual train crossing your path, just a few feet away, making its metallic rhythmic noise.

But three minutes of waiting? This is beyond health, beyond safety. A committee of control freaks appears to be intent on tamping down the efficiency of the populace, who need to get from A to B just as badly as the train does.

At long last – by which time you've ceased to care about the direction – the great rattling thing trundles along disappointingly slowly from left to right.

But the level crossing still doesn't go up. The red lights keep flashing. Now you feel panicky. Three more minutes? But, no, the second train always comes along pleasingly soon after the first one, always in the opposite direction, and this is somehow satisfying to your symmetrical urges.

No, please don't play the four movements of Brahms's Fourth Symphony

... in any old order, Spotify. And please don't call the movements 'your songs'. They're not 'songs', they're movements. And they need to be played in the right order.

Spotify just doesn't get it, with classical music. It thinks every separate item of music, if it has a spell of silence after it, can be played at any point on the 'shuffle' setting of the Spotify randomiser.

The period of time between the government announcing it's going to 'ban' something

... and the day on which they actually ban it is a strange, sad, emotionally charged time. Whether it's petrol, diesel, gas boilers, gas hobs, cigarettes, vapes, the sixth form without compulsory maths, driving at 30 mph, wood-burning stoves, logs in the fire or dogs on the beach, you live in a state of profound enjoyment of whatever it is that's been condemned to death, mingled with an effort to brace yourself for a bleak future without it.

'Ban.' Such a short word, but it carries with it acres of aching future loss.

July Screams

Please don't tell us which famous author's pen you used

. . . to sign the Book of Honour when you were elected as a Fellow of the Royal Society of Literature. 'I was honoured' . . . 'humbled' . . . 'delighted', 'I chose Jean Rhys's pen', 'I chose George Eliot's pen'; no one cares.

'Heavenly weekend having the grandchildren to stay'

(. . . and here's a photo of our prettiest granddaughter on one of our ponies, and by the way, in the background you can see our enormous garden, with a gate in the wall going through to another large bit of the garden, we call it the orchard, and you might just spot the corner of the swimming pool and more ponies in the field beyond. Yes, our grandchildren are a blessing and our life is perfect.)

Meanwhile, the Airbnb-ers are arriving in your street

You can hear their suitcases on wheels, coming to a halt. You look out and see the parents staring at their phone map and checking the house number, and the children gawping. They're probably Super-guests, arriving to stay chez the Super-host across the road.

You ought to feel nervous, because these strangers might be noisy, but your heart goes out to them. They're visibly relieved to have found the place to lay their heads. They ring the door-bell, and the Super-host comes down to greet them. This is life after hotels: holidays spent in normal residential areas, much more like real life, no Corby trouser press or mini-bar, and these people are getting to know the fascinating truth: what it's really like to live in YOUR ACTUAL AREA.

That very night, they have a screaming row

... in their twangy foreign language and you wish they'd get the hell out.

You feel an abiding sense of dread

... during the fortnight between admitting on the form that yes, it was you at the wheel, nipping through a traffic light 0.5 of a second after it went from amber to red – there's a photo to prove it, taken by one of the many police cameras spying on your entire life – and receiving the letter telling you precisely what the punishment will be.

What meanness

. . . that a large tub of cut-up pineapple and mango counts as a 'main' in a meal-deal. A tub of fruit is not a main course and never will be. What does the person who chooses it as a 'main' then have for 'afters'? A pack of Wotsits?

'I'm super-excited'

. . . says the international tennis star in her international English with the American accent.

What's wrong with 'very'? Just say 'very excited', please.

The horse chestnut trees

. . . look beautiful, in their full, astonishingly bright-green leaf, but on one single day in early July, every leaf of every single horse chestnut tree in Britain develops a small brown mark on it. Leaf-blotch. By mid-August, it will be deep autumn for those trees, and they'll never go a lovely autumnal colour: just straight from green to ill-brown. Are they gradually dying in this way, or will they always be allowed their exquisite spring before their unnaturally early autumn?

The large potted olive tree

. . . is still there on the pavement outside the nearby restaurant which has recently closed down, one of the hundreds of restaurants closing every week. Poor restaurant. Poor olive tree. Because you've been living so thriftily, the restaurant has gone from hubbub to desolation. You neither ate out nor helped out.

It didn't occur to the closers-down to take the potted olive tree with them when they closed down. With cigarette stubs scattered round its trunk, in its parched bit of soil, it stands there looking abandoned and forlorn, its status changed overnight from pet to stray.

You think back to a few weeks ago, when it was still living a pampered life, watered by people tipping away their unfinished Aperol spritzes, together with all the ice. Now the tree will need to rely solely on rainwater for its occasional drink. And it hasn't rained for three weeks. Are you allowed to take it home? Can you give a home to a rescue-tree?

A fox-pat

... has to be one of the most revolting-looking things in the urban world, when you find it on a hot summer's morning, all liquidy and brown at the corner of the street, up against a neighbour's wall. Yes, in the middle of the night, you heard the screeching of foxes who were having sex or killing something and their final act was for one of them to produce a small lake of fox diarrhoea.

Sash-style windows that don't open properly

... are a sad sight on a boiling afternoon in a shimmering city. They look like sash windows, but they're cheap replacements for what were once proper working sash windows with inbuilt rope and pulley – the kind of window that could go all the way up or down, allowing for half a windowful of fresh air.

The most these PVC ones can do is tip open a fraction, allowing a wisp of fresh air to drift in at the very top. To look at this is to be vicariously stifled.

The 'open here' perforations on a new box of cling film

... are so weird, so clever, so complicated, full of strange curves designed for an imagined dream scenario in which a kitchen goddess eases her unsnagged clingfilm out through a long narrow slit, that you can't make head or tail of them. The main aim at the cling-film box design conference must have been to enable customers to avoid the situation of having to pick away at a roll of narrowing cling film with their fingernails, trying to locate an 'end', because something went wrong a week and a half ago.

So, you're meant to push your index finger down between the perforations, are you, to make an elongated Poirot-moustache-shaped hole? And then pull out the thin piece of residue cardboard, as you would with a box of Kleenex? But as you jab your finger down, you make all kinds of new gashes at right angles to the perforations, and as you try to ease out the thin strip of cardboard, there's a tearing noise as a bits of the box come off too. For the next eighty metres of clingfilm, you'll have to revisit this wreck of a box and be reminded of your ineptitude.

The choice the computer gives you is 'install now'

... or 'install later today', or 'remind me tomorrow'. You don't want any of them. You're happy with the status quo.

You don't need anything new installed, and anyway the computer is probably too old to deal with the enforced change or update they're intending to inflict on it.

But you're not allowed to say 'no thanks'. 'Remind me tomorrow' is the least enthusiastic response they permit.

So you'll click 'remind me tomorrow' every day for the rest of your life, forever putting off the day.

But you did in fact book a holiday abroad

... and must now take your chance, along with half the population. All goes well until the moment when you're going through security, and you've done everything you've been told to do, taking off your shoes and belt and putting all liquids into the tiny plastic bag, and still your tray veers off down the wrong conveyor-belt pathway, the one along the back, behind the plate glass, out of reach – the 'in detention' conveyor belt for miscreants.

Someone wearing gloves opens it, displaying your pants to the strip-lit hall. They find a bar of soap which counts as 'liquid'.

Something utterly delicious to eat at the airport

It's astonishing how marvellous food can taste at an airport. They are places of unforgettable eating pleasure. It's partly

that you're in a psychological state of profound relief, grati-
tude and pride, for having got to this point: through customs
and security, 'airside', with the ideal fifty minutes to go till
boarding. Suddenly, hunger overwhelms you. And there's a
Pret, and a free table, and you have a voluminous cup of
coffee and an almond croissant so warm, flaky, moist and
sweet that you feel you're in heaven, even though you're in a
departure lounge within sight of a Watches of Switzerland
outlet.

The overhead lockers

. . . are full up by the time you enter the cabin. Of course
they are. Luggage is so expensive to check in that most
people travel as light as possible and bring their luggage
on board.

There's no room for your suitcase of the permitted
measurements in the locker above your seat, or anywhere
near it. What to do? Oh God, there's space in a locker
towards the back. So you'll have to put your suitcase in a
locker beyond where you'll be sitting, which will make for
a period of embarrassment and deep unpopularity when
the plane lands and everyone surges forward and you'll be
pushing backwards against the tide.

The film the man next to you on the plane is watching

... on his propped-up iPad looks dreadful. The man is wearing headphones, so all you have to go on are the visuals, but it's just wham, bam, car chase, exploding car, woman in high heels running for her life, ball of fire, ambulance hospital corridor, private room with slatted blinds, person on drip.

Do all films look this bad when you watch them on someone else's screen with the volume off? They do. Just as you are judging this person for his bad taste in unsubtle films, so you too will be judged by others surreptitiously observing your own choice of movie.

Buying nail scissors abroad

You have to, as of course you weren't allowed to bring nail scissors in your carry-on luggage. So you go to a foreign pharmacy and buy the pair of nail scissors, and they're fully visible but unreachable in the packet, ensconced in an impenetrable seamless thick-plastic factory-sealed pack, which you can't open because you haven't got any nail scissors.

The television in the hotel room

. . . is a large flat screen on the wall opposite the bed, which you're never going to watch, because these days everyone comes with their own laptop, so there's no need to work out how to use the remote control to watch foreign television with its cartoony commercial breaks every twelve minutes.

So the flat screen stays dead and black throughout your stay, a blot in the centre of your field of vision as you lie on the romantic bed. Couldn't they remove the television and replace it with a botanical print?

Salted caramel ice cream

This was the real reason you came abroad in the first place. Yes, you do love the walls, the piazzas, the steps up to the church at the top of the town, and the view, but with all your mind and all your body, what you most crave is the salted caramel ice cream: two scoops, served in a tub so there's no pollution from the dry wafer taste of a cone. The salty-sweet hit of this recently invented flavour is bliss, and you emit an audible yelp of pleasure in mid-year.

Foreign hotel basin plugs

... are a frustrating puzzle for the shaving man.

Is he supposed to pull the lever up or push it down, or is he supposed to use the index finger to push the plug down to make it first stay down and then push it again to make it jump up, or is he supposed just to use his fingernail, or (again) a pair of nail scissors to prise it back up and out? Nothing seems to work.

'Why can't they just have a simple good old black rubber plug on a chain?' he says.

You think you're running the bath while he's shaving. But you discover that the water has been steadily draining away for ten minutes, because the bathplug wasn't 'down' far enough, as you hadn't done it correctly.

Having had the bath, you then can't work out what you did to make the plug go down and stay down, so you can't work out how to do the opposite to let the water out. That's one for the cleaner.

Photographs of food on laminated menus in town squares

... are garish against the backdrop of the beautiful architecture. Sickly-yellow omelette. Orangey-gold chips. Tutti-frutti-coloured pizza. Scarlet spaghetti sauce. Turd-brown kebab. Every restaurant has exactly the same photos.

But you're weak with hunger and it all suddenly looks irresistible. You sink down at the one with the friendliest-looking waiter who brings you a carafe of wine and a basket of bread, and you're so relieved that you don't even mind that there's no butter so you have to pour olive oil onto the bread from the oil and vinegar cruets.

At the start of the journey home

. . . you arrive at the small airport to find that the plane you need to take hasn't yet taken off from its country of origin, let alone landed here, let alone been 'prepared' for your flight.

This is astonishing to contemplate. How can the vehicle you need to fly in still be on a runway a thousand miles away?

Where there should be a solid orange and white plane on the tarmac beyond your 'gate' waiting area, in which you will now be sitting for at least two and a half hours, there's nothing but a small forklift truck.

And, this being a small foreign airport in the evening, there's certainly no Pret and not even a restaurant, just a shop selling ready-salted crisps and warm orange juice.

It's time to play your favourite pop song on your Spotify playlist

... to cheer yourself up. So you find it, and ask it to play it, and it does. And you're back in your formative teenage years.

And then, when the song finishes, Spotify starts playing it all over again.

No, no, not again! You love it, but you don't love it that much.

August Screams

A strange Lego-like dinosaur-shaped creature appears on your screen along with the words 'Uh-oh! Something went wrong'

You are not cheered up, or comforted, or amused, by a Lego-like dinosaur-shaped creature at such a moment.

'In this hot weather, you are advised to carry water with you at all times'

So says the announcement on the tube station platform, and everyone frowns. No one thinks, 'Ah, thank you, good idea. I'll remember that next time.'

It's hydro-bullying. We know how to look after ourselves, thank you very much. We do not need a tannoy nanny. And there are quite enough plastic water bottles cluttering up the globe without every person going on the five million tube journeys per day needing to buy one to suck on at moments of possible faintness.

The bliss of driving when Google Maps

. . . is telling you exactly what to do and which way to go.

Yes, on balance, you've definitely got to love the satnav.

Once you've worked out how to start the journey (as with walking, 'head north along the B4079' doesn't help, and finding the initial right direction may take a while), layers of anxiety are lifted from your shoulders.

No more of the self-loathing, remorse and guilt that used to engulf you when you'd suggested the 'best route' and got stuck in traffic. No more of that fury and blame when your partner suggested his 'best route' and you got stuck in traffic. No more of the dreadful car-sickness induced by looking down at a heavy map book weighing on your thighs like a thick eiderdown.

Like a mixture between God and a really good nanny, Google Maps Knows Best. It even knows the names of every side street! Even in obscure villages and foreign towns! 'You're still on the fastest route,' the woman says, and this is what you need to know.

Knowing when you're going to arrive makes even a twelve-hour journey seem short. It inspires you to criss-cross Europe at weird angles, such as from Dresden to Barcelona ('includes tolls').

As a truth-teller, it's also an effective antidote to the journey times told to you by people who live in the country and want to lure you to visit them: 'We're only two hours from London.' Google Maps knows the truth. It's really two hours and fifty-one minutes.

Other people's recycling rules

'No, the kitchen paper goes in that one. It doesn't count as paper.' 'No, chicken bones go in that bucket.' 'No, teabags go in that smaller bucket, actually.' 'No, lids go in the lidded bin.' 'No, bottles go in the blue plastic box in the garage.' 'No, plastic goes in the green box.' Trying to help other people in their kitchens, you cause real offence.

And the revoltingness of their recycling bucket!

The normal thing you'd hope to do when discarding unwanted food is to tip it into a large bin, deep and dark enough (thanks to the black bin liner) that you don't have to watch it land.

Here, there's a 'special small recycling bucket' for food, provided by the council, and 'special recyclable bags' to go inside it. It's a grey bucket and the condom-thin bags have the helpful word 'OPEN' at one end, where you need to rub it together to prise the two sides apart.

First, you put in half a loaf of their mouldy sliced bread. Then you need to get rid of a third of a salad bowlful of curried sweetcorn, chicken and mayonnaise which you've been living on for the last two days but has now gone off a bit.

But there's no tipping it into the depths, with this small recycling bucket. You have to spoon everything from the salad bowl into the small bag, watching as spoonful after spoonful of yellow and beige globules land on top of the mouldy bread. The bag almost overflows with this vomit-like concoction, and then there are two banana skins to add to the top, and you then have to take the bag out of the small bucket, tie a knot with the ends you can get hold of, and put the whole soft, heavy, damp thing into the much larger green council food bucket in the garage, to be emptied into the recycling lorry in five days' time. There's a heatwave on. You open the larger bucket and it's crawling with tiny white worm-like organisms.

This is how every summer lunch ends, at this house.

But their kitchen drawers

. . . designed by an expensive kitchen designer, are marvellous! Covetable! Their pale-grey cutlery drawer does the delicious thing of pausing just before closing, and then quietly and steadily, in its own good time, closing to perfection. This is known as the 'soft-close mechanism'. 'So you never need to

slam *the drawers shut!' your host patiently explains, in a slightly loud voice, after you first try doing exactly that.*

This mechanical action brings all the silence and gentleness of the 'soft-close' lavatory seat to the kitchen zone, and is a wonder of the modern age.

'34 per cent chance of rain'

... says the BBC Weather app for the area, just as you're planning to go for a long afternoon walk in an 'unsettled' week in August when the country seems to be permanently stuck on the wrong side of the great U-bend of the jet stream.

So, do you go or not go for the walk?

Thirty-four per cent is about the most tricky percentage to deal with. Anything over 50 per cent, and you won't go for the walk. That would be asking for trouble. Anything below 33 and you would probably go. (However badly you ever did in a school science exam, the mark was never below 33. That would be an embarrassingly low percentage.)

But 34 per cent? Does that mean there's just over a one-in-three chance that you will get soaked, or does it mean that you'll get soaked for just over a third of the walk?

It's actually more unhelpful than helpful to be given this particular nugget of mathematical probability.

Back home, and you can't get the last little bit of mayonnaise

... out of the Hellmann's squeezy bottle. Those bottles are designed to withhold their last remnants so you can't reach them, and are left gagging for more.

However small the spoon, it won't turn a right angle when it gets below the rim, to reach the stuff stuck on the circular ledge. You put the lid back on and bang it and bang it upside down, but still nothing shifts. Someone else has squeezed the bottle so hard that there's now a permanent cinch in the middle, so it's no longer even a squeezy bottle; it's now just a squeezed bottle.

So there's nothing for it. You have to rinse out the whole bottle in hot water, shaking it to dislodge the mayonnaisey residue which turns the water into pale milky liquid. One more minor domestic act to turn the stomach.

The un-deadheaded roses

... in the front garden of your new neighbours (who are renting, so probably don't care and clearly don't know a thing about gardening) are driving you mad, with their neglected remnants of roses where their flowers were a fortnight ago. The poor things would flower a second time, if only these idiots would deadhead them, or if only you could be let loose on them with your secateurs. Like the potted olive tree, that rose tree is crying out for love and attention. But would the new neighbours think you dotty, nosy, invasive and intrusive if you said to them, 'Do you mind if I deadhead your roses?' They would.

You can't right all the wrongs of the floral world.

Pale tomatoes

If you don't grow your own, so you aren't one of the people posting photos of their crop, whether it be large ('bumper year!') or small ('just three cherry tomatoes this year!'), you're stuck with buying the things. Since the invention of the 'Finest' range and the 'on the vine' range, where you get nine flawless red tomatoes at an extortionate price, 'normal' tomatoes have gone right downhill. It's like what happened to secondary moderns when there was a grammar school next door.

The 'normal' tomatoes – the ones that don't say 'Finest' or 'on the vine' – are horribly inferior. They're pale orange and hard. Just looking at them, you know they'll never 'home-ripen' and will be almost flavourless, even when fried, even when you add sugar as well as salt and pepper.

'Swim in poo '

... says the funny sign to a swimming pool you see online, of which some of the letters have been blanked over, but it's all too true when it comes to today's seawater. It's just about swimmable-in where you are, except for the patches of stinking dark-green seaweed and the rumours of jellyfish, but further round the coast, the water is a much darker brown than the usual sand-brown, and must be avoided, and crowds of boiling-hot people are sitting on the sand not daring to go in.

'No worries'

... says the neighbour when you tell him that no, sadly, you don't have a long ladder to lend him. He's English, but when he says that, he sounds Australian.

And then you start listening to the cricket match, and the commentators sound Australian too. 'It's a Maximum.'

No, it's not. It's what we would call a 'six'.

Oh God, now it's dahlias

... that the people with big walled gardens are showing us photos of on social media. First it was their crop of daffodils, then it was tulips, then the roses, and now it's dahlia-boast fortnight (with a side-order of home-grown courgettes in a basket).

Enormous yellow dahlias as large as hedgehogs with a thousand pointy petals; deep purple and deep pink ones from their herbaceous border; all plonked together into three vases on their kitchen table with the Aga on its summer setting in the background.

The message: 'Living in the countryside has its ups and downs, but this is one of the ups and I'm going to rub your noses in it.'

And then you can't resist a little boast of your own

... a photo of your own candlelit table laid for supper, displaying your own exquisite taste and your good fortune to be living where you do. And a little part of your soul dies as you publish this boast.

And then, for Chrissakes, only eight people 'like' it. You've sold your soul for eight 'likes'.

The final bars of the first movement

... of Beethoven's 'Emperor' Piano Concerto are playing at the Proms. 'Please don't clap. Please don't clap,' you pray.

But as soon as the final chord of the first movement ends, the Royal Albert Hall erupts in applause.

It's not the Prommers standing in the central arena who are clapping. They're proper, cash-strapped music lovers, who wouldn't dream of clapping after the first movement. It's the affluent people in the expensive seats: the ones who probably wouldn't have a clue about the answers to the classical music round on *University Challenge*.

They want to show their approval of the loud music, and some of them even shout, 'Bravo!' Oh God. It's embarrassing. The orchestra doesn't react to the clapping or the cheering. The conductor doesn't turn round, or bow. Within about seven seconds, the clappers get the message that they've done a Wrong Thing, and their clapping fades out as suddenly as it began.

Interestingly, they only do this clapping at the end of the loud movements. At the end of quiet ones, such as slow movements, they remain silent.

Absolute favourite words on a digital board at a railway station

'On time.'

Those words are so beautiful, so perfectly in tune with how you want the world of travel to be, that you read them and reread them. On time. On time. On time.

The person in front of you at the supermarket checkout

... is on her mobile phone, on speakerphone, throughout the transaction. Doesn't even look at the checkout operator's face, or speak to him or notice him or thank him. Tries to pay with her phone, while speaking, but it won't connect. Searches her wallet for her debit card, while still on the phone. Frustrated, annoyed, flustered, can't find it, eventually does find it, but as she does so, all her cards fall out onto the floor, a wonderful sight, and you're not going to help her pick them up, as she's still on the phone. May she live in a perpetual state of chaotic distraction, so absent from the present moment that she's absent from her own life.

September Screams

'Oh no! You're acronym blind!'

The cargo bikes are out in force

... ridden by local mothers displaying their eco-credentials as they ferry their broods to their new school and nursery on the golden early days of the autumn term.

You can be pretty certain, judging from their tans, that these families have just flown back from their villa holiday in Italy. And now here they are, flaunting their net-zero existence. In order to live this cargo-bike life, they must have very wide entrance halls or ample off-street parking. Or they park the vast eco-vehicle on the pavement outside their house, covered in an enormous waterproof hood.

They certainly have entitled, lazy children lording it in the front compartment, who prefer not to walk two-thirds of a mile.

What used to be the beloved local Italian restaurant

... has closed down over the summer and become a Five Guys. The bay you used to sit in, all those years ago, tucking in to the scalding 'lasagne al forno' in its untouchably hot metal dish, chatting, glugging the house red, falling in love, is now the ketchup-pump and stirrers area of this new outlet of the fast-food chain.

After a week in the English countryside

... you return to the dismal selection of supermarket flowers. They're all horrible, with much-too-long stems, which might make them last but also makes them too tall for any known household vase. Overpoweringly scented lilies. Too-bright gladioli: someone else's idea of 'a riot of colour'. Wispy little freesias with all their petals too low down, so if you did cut the stems there'd be hardly any flowers left on them. Prim bunches of tight pinks. Bunches of twelve perfect 'gift' roses which might, just might, last five days if you smashed the stems with a hammer and then tipped out the sachet of Alka-Seltzer-like 'cut-flower food'.

Bought flowers are another species entirely from normal, blowy, real flowers of the garden.

'Please let me know which of these dates you can do'

... writes the organising friend from the former school mothers' group to everyone in the WhatsApp group, 'and let's hope there's a date that suits us all.' She offers five different Wednesday and Thursday evenings over the next two months.

So, here goes: the game of 'who's the busiest?' You look at your diary and see that you're free on every evening she suggests. Do you dare admit as much? Or do you say, 'I can do every date except 17 Oct', otherwise they'll think you're the saddest person ever, to be so completely un-booked up, so totally non-theatre-going, and so plainly uninvited-out.

You decide to stick your neck out. 'I can do any of those dates.'

One says, 'I can only do 9 or 10 Oct', thereby instantly reducing the pool of possible dates to two.

One says, 'I can only do 16 or 17 Oct', so there's now no middle bit of the Venn diagram.

One says, 'I can't do any of those dates. V booked up at end of Sept, and going to LA in Oct. So sorry! Can you suggest some other possibilities?'

Organiser has to start all over again. Possible dates now start in late Oct and stretch on into late Nov.

You look at your diary. Wonderfully, you have got something in the diary for one of the suggested dates! Proudly, nonchalantly, you reply, 'I can do any of these dates except 7 Nov.'

The only date everyone can do is the one at the very end of Nov. Will you all even be still alive by the time the great day arrives?

The hen-night ladies on the train

... are drawing attention to themselves, with their loud voices, matching pink skimpy tulle dresses, enormous bare thighs, feet stuffed into stilettos, mascara, foundation and blusher loaded on with their various applicators, pink hairbands, strappy shoulder bags digging into fleshy shoulders, dinky shopping bags from Victoria's Secret showing off their pre-hen-night spree.

The poor things will soon get out and will have to totter to the venue in the drizzle, feet in agony, only to be plied with sickly-sweet cocktails for hours on end and then miss the last train home.

It's so lovely not being one of them that this whole encounter turns into a guilty pleasure.

'Your parcel is now with your local Evri courier for delivery'

So exciting, even though it's just contact lenses for another family member. But it's nice to hear the email pinging in, telling you that something is even now winging its way towards you, feeling the magnetic pull of your dwelling.

Lying awake at night

. . . you try to remember what the latest collection of letters is. Is it 'LGBTQIA'? Has it still got a plus-sign at the end? It has. The plus sign implies 'infinite possibilities, so don't take offence if we've left one category out'.

Then you try to make a word out of it, as it's currently seven letters, like a Scrabble hand. Tricky, as there's no 'U' to go with the 'Q'. So you start thinking of a category that would begin with a 'U'.

And then you lie awake frightened half to death

. . . contemplating that if you say one 'inappropriate' thing, or 'misgender' someone, or even support someone supporting someone else you happen to agree with, and are therefore cancelled by the online mob, your hair will turn white overnight and will come out in great handfuls when you brush it, you'll turn into a gaunt waif, your career will be over, your life wrecked, and you might as well die there and then.

And you think about the word 'cancelled'

It's bad enough on an airport departure board on a day of countrywide IT failure: 'cancelled', 'cancelled', 'cancelled', 'go to gate 10', 'cancelled', 'cancelled'. But what if you yourself were cancelled? That would be worse. Airbrushed from history. Liquidated. You'd be missed for a few weeks, but the ripples would quickly close over you.

All you would pray for in your miserable, isolated, cancelled exile would be that the cancellers would one day themselves be cancelled for having cancelled you.

That's it for cashmere jerseys – never again!

They don't even last a year. Don't be tempted by one this autumn. Yes. Look. The beautiful cashmere jersey you were given last Christmas, and the ones you gave, costing an absurd £125 each because you bought them before the January sales, are now unwearable after the summer: riddled with moth holes in the middle, and the holes of a badly sewn jersey at the sewn junctures, where they're literally falling apart at the seams. They are a bitter disappointment.

'How was your delivery?'

The package arrived, exactly in the way that posted, paid-for and delivered items have since the idea of posting things began. Nothing more needs to be said on the subject. Take no news as good news, please.

Which direction are you supposed to go in

... when you enter Room 3 of the new autumn block-buster exhibition? There's clearly disagreement about this, because when you cram in to Room 3, crowding round to have a proper look at the famous picture on the first wall on the left – so significant that it certainly does have a 'headphone' sign, meaning 'whatever you do, don't miss this one', people are coming at it from both directions.

Some think you should turn left as a matter of course when you go into any room of a blockbuster exhibition. Turn left, and continue round the room clockwise. That is instinctive.

But what if the placard about Room 3 – the long slab of prose in italics on the wall, explaining the room's theme, such as 'The Seville Years' or 'Experiments with light, 1929–1935' – is on the right as you enter the room, rather than the left? Surely, then, you should set off past the placard and onwards in an anticlockwise direction?

Nobody knows. Nobody tells you. So there are collisions and outbreaks of crossness as people converge on each other in frowning silence.

'I wish I knew about these fitted sheets sooner'

... says the online advertisement that knows you're looking for a new fitted sheet. It's quoting a supposed satisfied customer. What on earth happened to the pluperfect?

Please stop laughing your heads off, podcast presenters

You're finding it extremely funny as you tease each other and joke-criticise each other for the first ten minutes of your podcast, like a married couple at a weekend house party. But we're not finding it at all funny and wish you'd pipe down and get on with the business of discussing whichever aspect of slavery it is that you're focusing on in Episode 3 of your series on slavery.

'Fry the onions, then add the chicken'

Nope. Doesn't work. You need to take the onions out before adding the chicken, otherwise the onions will burn and the chicken won't brown.

So many recipes seem not to take account of the requirements of actual cooking.

'Fry the chicken for two minutes on each side'

Nope. Doesn't work. It'll still be pink inside and give you salmonella poisoning. Why are these male chef authors in such a frantic hurry?

'The woman who gave me my medical

... was really nice, actually,' says the partner, who gets a free medical with work, 'and she said I should try to eat dark-green-leaf vegetables at least five times a week.'

In order to conform with this recommendation, the easy balance of how many dark-green-leaf vegetables you would naturally eat each week gets unnaturally upset, and everyone gets a tummy ache.

'Did you ever hear back about that job you applied for?'

'No.'

It's the silence that's so dreadful. At least, in the olden days, people got a proper typed rejection letter: 'We're very sorry, but due to the exceptionally high calibre of applicants, we regret that we are unable to offer you a job at this juncture, but we'll keep your name on our files.'

That was no fun to receive, but at least you knew

your name was 'on their files'. Someone might flick through those files one day and find it. This silence, this Bermuda Triangle into which the whole concept of you vanishes, is worse. The people so rude that they can't be bothered to write rejection letters are making the ones at the receiving end of the rudeness and silence feel unwanted, unnoticed, unneeded, superfluous to the world's requirements.

Assorted masks

... still lying about at home, which you keep coming across by accident – under the box in the hall, under the basin, used as bookmarks or at the bottom of drawers – make you shudder.

There's the one you were first sent as early as April 2020, made by an enterprising schoolgirl when the schools were first closed, who sold them on a wall in her village, but she hadn't yet learned that masks needed pleats in order to expand adequately for the nose. So that was a suffocating mask.

There's the pale-blue disposable one you bought in a pack of ten and wore before it became fashionable to wear masks made of proper material, and unfashionable to wear the disposable kind known as 'face nappies'.

Then there's the black one you picked up at the counter of the hairdresser's when they first opened again and you had the first appointment after an unbelievably long time. The white string of that one went brown, and it wasn't the dirt behind your ears. It was the semi-permanent 'veg tint'.

There's the 'Titian' one you succumbed to in the gift shop at the first exhibition you were allowed to go to when museums opened again. It seemed so witty and charming at the time.

There's the hard, white, surgical-style one you were forced to buy from the tourist shop in the Italian town in order to be allowed to go on an outdoor boat on a lake.

There's the exquisite, non-itchy paisley one you were given by your most chic friend.

There's the no-frills flesh-coloured one you ordered from John Lewis, one of a pack of three. The flesh colour made you look as if you had no mouth.

You don't dare throw any of these hideous items away, because you flatly refuse ever to spend another penny on the ghastly things in your life, but what if they ever become 'mandatory' again? God forbid.

Afternoon Tea

You're going out to one, and it costs £39.25 each, which isn't bad in comparison to the one at the swankiest hotel where Afternoon Tea 'starts at' £72 per person and is called The Afternoon Tea Experience, and costs much more if you include a glass of champagne, and people are still gorging on their scones at 9 p.m. in the specially designated Afternoon Tea menagerie off the palm court.

But still, this Afternoon Tea (it always has capital letters) at 3.30 totally messes up the day's meals. You can't have any lunch, as you're going to be going out to tea in two hours' time, and after the tea you'll feel bloated at 5.30 p.m., which will wreck the prospect of supper.

But the tiers!

They're dazzling. It's the three-tiered cake stand that makes Afternoon Tea an irresistible concept and a treat of the modern age. When the waiter arrives carrying the absurdly tall structure, as madly, generously outsized as the bouquet of flowers the leading soprano is presented with during her opera curtain call, you can only gasp with wonder and gratitude.

It's the joy of the rocket shape, the spire shape, the Christmas-tree shape. It's the bliss of there being THREE tiers. Sober sandwiches on the bottom, rising, via scones and accompanying ramekins of cream and jam, to fairy-tale pink, mousse-style showstopper miniatures on the top.

'Afternoon Tea.' It's a racket. No one needs this amount to eat in the afternoon. And they never give you enough tea to drink with it. You have to plead for 'some more hot water' and hope they won't charge you. But the tiers live on in your phone's memory as well as yours.

'Please may I use your loo?'

… you ask the man behind the counter at the next-door bookshop, which doesn't actually have any customer toilets. But this man is kind. And he knows you might buy a book once you've been to the loo. So he says, 'Yes, do use the staff one. It's just through that door on the left.'

And you go in there – and it's extremely shabby. This is truly 'behind the scenes in the bookshop', the part the public doesn't see. A pile of stacked folding chairs, a mop, a broom, a dustpan and brush, a grimy basin and a grubby white hand towel.

At first, it's a bit of a shock, and you think, 'So, this is how they treat the staff.' But then it starts to seem homely, the only homely place in the shop, in fact, with its cleaning utensils and the brown ring on the basin where someone recently placed their cup of Nescafé. If you worked in this bookshop you'd hang out in here quite a lot.

Mac 'n' cheese

Is the 'n' in the middle meant to be the 'n' in the middle of 'and', or is it meant to be the 'n' in the middle of 'macaroni'? Whatever it is, it looks ridiculous, especially if the first of the inverted commas is a forward-facing open-quote rather than the correct backward-facing close-quote.

It's not 'mac and cheese', for goodness' sake. It's

'macaroni cheese' and is usually pretty disgusting, except on the rare occasion when it's home-made by a roux-expert whose oven-baked offerings don't taste like boarding-school Saturday supper.

'Me'

'Also me.'

This is a post in which someone gives us two contrasting photographs of himself which illustrate the fascinating paradox in his character. 'Me': a photo of him going out for a run at the crack of dawn. 'Also me': a photo of him conked out, fast asleep on the sofa.

God, he finds himself so intriguing and amusing.

Magsafe 2?

Is that the computer cable you need? But in the photo, one of its ends seems to be slightly different from the kind of end that will plug into the kind of socket you already have.

It's hard enough to find the 'cables and chargers' section inside the 'accessories' section inside the 'shop now' section in the first place. Once you do, there are far too many of them, ranging from cutting edge to just about obsolete, and the prices are scarily varied: you can get the thing you think you might be looking for for £19.99, but that only has 774 customer reviews and a three-and-a-half-star rating, whereas a similar-looking one costs £79.00 and has 4,551 customer reviews and a four-star rating. Still not five stars. Something is clearly still a bit wrong with it.

Squidging rice packets

It's lazy to go down the route of ready-cooked rice. But it's sometimes irresistible, because you crave the sensation of squidging the packet before putting it into the microwave, having first snipped off its top corner, as the instructions say you must. The packet goes from rock-hard to soft as you squeeze it – the same sublime sensation as opening a rigid pack of Illy ground coffee and feeling it sigh into softness. You'd think 'squidging to make something go from hard to soft' would be an unsexy sensation, but for some reason it's exactly the opposite.

'Please step away from your bake'

The release of tension at the moment when these words are spoken on *The Great British Bake-Off* is felt by the entire viewing population, as well as by the stressed-out contestants.

But 'bake' as a noun? Shouldn't that be 'please step away from your cake'?

But it's Bread Week. So they have to call it a bake.

The rot set in with the 'cheesy pasta bake' of the 1980s.

'You've completely caught up'

So says your social media feed. What it means is 'stop scrolling, you sad person. There's nothing new to see. You only checked it two minutes ago and nothing has since changed. None of your friends, in the last two minutes, has had anything interesting to boast. Go and get a life.'

October Screams

*'It's amazing how long he can go on
talking about his electric car's range.'*

This morning's 'Small Litter'

... in the first five minutes of stepping out of the house: empty triangular BLT sandwich container. Squished Red Bull can. Black plastic box that someone's sushi came in, with the empty miniature squeezy bottle beside it. Bag of KFC bones to choke passing dog to death. Pink prawn cocktail crisp packet. Snickers wrapper. Rothmans packet showing large photo of yellow teeth and cancerous lung. Diet Coke bottle.

What was going through the mind of the dropper of each of these at the moment they let them go? Nothing, perhaps. No thought, no awareness, no twinge of guilt. They were in your area but cared this little for its beauty.

There's only one thing to do: sing Mr Craddock the Park Keeper's lyrics from the 1960s 'Watch with Mother' show *Trumpton*, the sweetly exasperated song he sang as he went about with his litter-picking stick. You could set about picking up the rubbish yourself, like Mr Craddock, but would that be the first step to becoming a bag lady?

The stillborn photograph album

It stopped, suddenly, one day in 2011. That was the date when you ceased to stick any photos into the album, and just kept all photos on the phone and computer instead.

Your descendants will now know nothing about your life from that day on, because they're certainly not going to be trawling through your phone photos, of which there are far too many of the same events, after you die.

The day came in 2011 when, for the last time in your life, you went to the chemist's to collect prints. Such an exciting moment, when you got hold of the yellow packet of still-warm photos and were so impatient to look at them that you did it right there, outside the chemist's shop, dazzled by the images of your life and family and friends glamorised and immortalised in 5x7-inch 'matt'.

Then came the glue-scented afternoon, when for the last time you sat and stuck the photos in, cropping them to fit, discarding half of them, and writing the captions.

Now the album goes blank after the last happy stuck-in event of 2011: summer, trees, children, smiling, fountain, waves, then just empty white pages.

'I'm feeling heavy-hearted about the terrible events

... going on in [whichever foreign country has just ex-
perienced the appalling horror that's dominating the
headlines]. But I find deep solace in walking with my dog,
in my fields and orchards, reminding me that the natural
rhythms of life carry on and the world keeps turning ...'
Oh do shut up.

'Jesus will arrive in four minutes'

So posts the person who has just ordered an Uber, and he
shows you the photo of that very message on his phone, together with the quip, 'I didn't expect the Second Coming
quite this soon'.

It was only funny the first time. Jesus is not such a rare
name in the Uber-driving population.

It's getting colder, so the poor shivering mouse

... is desperate to come and live indoors with you. And it
does. But you can't be expected to cohabit with a mouse
excreting all over the chopping board.

The new mouse poison, to comply with current strict
standards, is too weak to kill a mouse outright. So the
tiny creature emerges from under the kitchen work surface

every evening for a fortnight, looking slower, more lost, more distressed and more ill each time. You feel dreadful about its long-drawn-out death.

'Who gives a crap?'

Who gives a crap? Who gives a crap? Who gives a crap? Who gives a crap?' The 'Who gives a crap?' loo rolls, each wrapped up in different-coloured sustainable wrapping paper (isn't that a bit wasteful of paper?), are piled high in friends' loos, each one labelled 'Who gives a crap?' Yes, these people clearly do give a crap and want to tell us they buy loo paper not made from trees and loo paper whose profits go to help people without loos in the developing world. It's wonderful, but who gives a crap?

'Four-way control'

. . . says the red sign. This is one of the grim three-worders, along with 'rail replacement bus' and 'wait in hall'. Four-way control means a very long wait at a traffic light. Of course, nothing much is coming in any of the other directions. But you have to sit it out, waiting for one imaginary stream of traffic to do its forty seconds, then the next from one side road, and then the next from the other side road, until, eventually, the man you imagine in a sentry box with godlike powers, who presses the buttons to change the lights, decides that, yes, he might now allow you to proceed.

Petrol or diesel?

Feeling frazzled at the end of a long day, standing beside the nozzles on the service station forecourt, you briefly can't remember which it is. Having owned a diesel car for ten years, because you were told a few prime ministers ago that it was good for the planet, you trained yourself to remember: 'Diesel. Diesel. Diesel. The one with the black handle. Diesel. Don't forget.'

It's at these moments – tired, absent-minded, thinking about other things such as the saddest child, who you are only ever as happy as – that you're most at risk of making the terrible mistake. Because now you own a petrol car again, to avoid the new excessive charges, and it's harder to unlearn something than to learn it. You're still trying to un-learn 'Diesel' and re-learn 'Petrol'. 'Petrol. Petrol. Petrol. The one with the green handle. Petrol. Don't forget.'

If and when you do make the mistake and unleash 50 litres of the wrong fuel into the tank, it's as bad as accidentally giving chocolate to the dog. You have to put your whole life on hold, there and then, while it waits to have its stomach pumped.

If you ever get an electric vehicle, will you be spotted pitifully trying to charge it up with a petrol nozzle?

'It's actually got quite a good range'

... says the acquaintance who has bought an electric vehicle – or EV as he calls it – and is being evangelical about it.

'Of course, we're lucky, because we've got our own off-street parking space so we can just plug it in and keep it charging all night. And it can go 290 miles on one charge.'

'So does that mean you have to stop somewhere for the night on the way to Scotland to charge it up?'

'Yeah, but you factor that into the journey. It's actually really nice stopping for a night on the way. Makes the whole journey more leisurely and enjoyable, somehow. And if anything goes wrong with the car and you break down, the car's own computer instantly alerts the head office.'

Sounds like a total nightmare.

It looked like a small puddle on the narrow country lane

... down which the satnav has sent you, but was in fact a pothole disguised as a puddle. Your non-EV car makes a small, sudden lurch to the front-left.

It's a flat tyre.

But, hooray, you are a member of the AA! And with your customary efficiency, you have the card in your wallet to prove it.

After the lengthy safety spiel, during which you have to admit you're not in any kind of immediate danger, they pinpoint your location in the middle of muddy nowhere and tell you they'll be along in an hour and a half's time. Could be a lot worse. Time to listen to a podcast and a half.

But now you have an hour and a half to worry about one thing: where are the locking wheel nuts?

If you can't find the locking wheel nuts – whatever they are, but they're absolutely essential – this situation will be disastrous. The man won't be able to unlock the tyre, and you'll have to be towed away, but to where, because who'll be open after dark, and who in the world has your locking wheel nuts?

Inevitably, they're not in the glove compartment, where they should be. Nor in any of the side pockets. Nor tucked into the black nylon holder which contains the instruction manual – which *is* in the glove compartment, along with the migraine pills.

It's all so deeply worrying that you can't fully concentrate on the first podcast or the first half of the second.

At last, along comes the yellow van

. . . a 'happiness' trigger as powerful as that of a taxi with its yellow light on, and you're cradled in the yellow safety of the rescue operation.

The man takes the filthy bags of walking boots and gumboots out of the boot and opens a trapdoor underneath, and there, deep down in one of five small compartments, inside a thick polythene bag, are the locking wheel nuts! Ecstasy floods through your body.

You were also sort-of worried that you didn't have a spare tyre, but of course, these days, no one has a proper spare tyre. The man just gives you the temporary one that lives in the car: enough to tide you over till you get to the local garage. And who cares if you have to spend the whole of tomorrow searching for a garage in a village of which you know nothing? You found the locking wheel nuts!

It's only 10 October, and already

. . . Halloween cobwebbery is draped over front railings, looking bedraggled, because it's pouring with rain.

It's bad enough that in this very same week, the 'Christmas Shop' assaults you when you enter the local department store, fake trees glittering across the ground floor. Who are the weirdos who want to start buying Christmas trees on 10 October?

You can sort of see that some people, perhaps especially tourists, might get excited about Christmas two and a half months early and might want to pick up a fake tree to take back home.

But to be this pre-excited about . . . Halloween?

The cheap folding umbrella

. . . which you buy at the first chemist you pass, in order to deal with the sudden downpour, works for precisely six seconds before the first sharp gust of wind turns it inside out and snaps two of its spokes, so when you manage to wrestle it back from convex to concave, two of what should be its pointy edges hang down limply, like broken dog's paws or a limp handshake.

As 'named storms' are getting stronger and more frequent, umbrellas are getting weaker at precisely the same rate.

The bliss of walking past a sodden rugby pitch

. . . at 2 p.m. on a freezing, rainy October weekday afternoon, with (now) an enormous, sturdy 'golfing'-type umbrella that does work (even though it doesn't have a round bend at the bottom to hold, just a vertical phallic rubbery end to clutch), wearing a lovely warm coat, and not having to be one of the

schoolchildren playing rugby on that semi-waterlogged pitch! This is the cream of adulthood. The way to suck the most joy out of the sight is to think back to your own schooldays, when you did have to play games in the driving rain on most weekday afternoons, wearing skimpy games clothes, being screamed at by the games teacher, and 'letting the whole team down' with terrible passing mistakes on the rare occasions when you encountered the ball.

These poor darlings are doing exactly this, in shorts, right now, just a few metres away on the other side of the fence. A bully in a tracksuit is roaring at them, and they're all running in a great herd across the mud, heaving themselves towards the ball.

So are you going to go for

… the spaghetti with bacon, mushrooms and cream at 950 calories, or the steak and ale pie and chips at 1,072 calories, or would it be more sensible to stick with the roast cauliflower with cumin at just 442 calories?

It has to be the roast cauliflower – which is actually a dismal choice. But calorie numbers on menus are so powerful that they trump the words and outweigh all other considerations. You couldn't live with yourself if you chose the 950-calorie item you really want.

Visiting a beloved elderly friend in hospital

... the nurse at the entrance to the ward glances up at the chart and tells you that your friend is in Bay 3 on the left. So you go to Bay 3 on the left, but the person in bed doesn't quite look like your friend. She has grey hair like the friend, but somehow looks different, older, scraggier. You go a bit closer. Perhaps she's so ill that she really does look like this now? You go closer still. The old lady is staring back at you, perhaps lonely and bewildered and hoping for a visitor. Oh, God, it's definitely not her. It's suddenly scary, as if your friend no longer exists, and has been replaced by this different old person who looks extremely thin and ill. You have to say, 'Hello – oh, I'm so sorry, I've come to see someone else.'

All because the overstretched nurse told you the wrong bay.

'OPEN. Opening hours: 10–6'

You've checked online. So, it's open! Hooray! And you drive all the way there.

But not only is it not open, it has permanently closed down.

Watching the BBC Weather forecast

It's marvellous that you can now watch the BBC Weather at any time of day. It's a perpetual comfort-watch, even if, or perhaps especially if, the weather's deteriorating. Get under the duvet at 3.30 p.m., tune into the weather, and treat yourself to two minutes of profound relaxation.

No point in just watching the local forecast for your area. Where's the fun in that? You need the sweeping national picture: what it's going to be like in Stornoway, Aberdeen, 'across the Pennines', in mid-Wales and at Land's End. You gaze at the charming, bland, slightly geeky, meteorologically obsessed forecaster in smart indoor clothes as he or she prepares you for the next twenty-four hours in the parallel universe of the dreadful weather, all dictated by forces thirty miles up in the sky, utterly indifferent to your plans.

So mesmerising is it that it's easy to miss the important detail of exactly what it's going to be like for you tomorrow. You watch the projected weather front as it curls round the whole country in a wispy circle like a dog chasing its tail. Curly weather, and you're somewhere in the middle of it.

November Screams

'Oh no! 9,999 steps to go!'

Don't show us your Wordle result

... with the green squares near the top denoting how quickly you solved it today. We're not interested.

And don't show us your positive Covid test with the two red lines, irrefutable proof that you've actually got the famous disease. We know it feels like a minor triumph, like a positive pregnancy test, except that you didn't have to DO anything to get it.

We're not interested.

A famous person's death is announced at 10.30 a.m.

... and everyone you've heard of, as well as everyone you've never heard of, instantly gets to work on social media, ostensibly to express their condolences, but really to latch on to the freshly dead person, saying how they

163

once met the person, and once had professional dealings with the person, and how nice the person was about them in particular, and how deeply they'll miss the person, and may the person rest in peace, and by the way, here's a photograph of them with the person.

'Did you see the YouTube video of the man shooting his printer to pieces on the lawn?'

. . . is the only thing to say while watching the frustrated family member struggling with the home printer, which claims to be 'jammed'.

You long to take yours out into the garden and shoot it, but you don't keep firearms like the man in the YouTube video did. So instead, you have to open its strange back end and reach your forearm, vet-like, inside its back passage to try to locate any corner of the jammed paper you can get a hold of, and then do your best to tug it out gently enough that you don't tear it and thus leave half of it inside.

The printer lets you down well over half the time anyone tries to use it. When you press 'print', you're amazed if everything goes smoothly. It's as rare as taking a moody toddler out to a country house hotel restaurant and avoiding some kind of tantrum or meltdown.

Best episode yet of Grand Designs

... *because the 'morass of mud' week is particularly dire for the couple doing the 'new build'. It's a quagmire out there, in the plot in the field where the contractors are trying to lay the foundations for the enormous steel-framed dream home.*

The couple are standing there in their hard hats in the rain, in a kind of despair, as today's digger can't even get up the drive. Then you see the husband with his head in his hands, staring at his computer in the caravan where the couple are currently living with their two small children, toys all over the place, and this part of the project has already been going on for longer than expected and the costs are rising 'exponentially'.

It's for this schadenfreude *that we watch such programmes; not for the drooling final five minutes when the couple are dressed in their best and welcome us in to their cavernous new kitchen with its plate-glass window offering a panoramic view.*

'Jason, Sue and all at J. W. Security

... wish you a happy Diwali.'
It's an e-card from the burglar-alarm company, with a photo of three candles burning brightly on a table in a darkened room. You can click on the photo to enlarge it.
Neither Jason nor Sue, nor anyone at J. W. Security, has

thought of you personally when mass-sending this e-card to all their clients via the 'bcc' method. Not a single well-wishing emotion has been expended by anyone towards you, and you certainly have no intention of expending a well-wishing emotion back towards them.

When it comes to the actual burglar alarm

... all you need is for the '2' on the keypad to work properly. When you arrive home and jab the keypad, it's supposed to emit a beep for each jab, but in the deafening din of the thirty-second noise that's supposed to give burglars half a minute to scarper before the alarm goes off, you can't hear whether it has beeped or not, so you press '2' again, and again, and this causes confusion and havoc, as well as wearing out the '2', and the thirty seconds are up all too soon, and the alarm goes off with a terrible wailing scream, and the keypad now displays an 'E-2' message which can only mean 'error, type-2'.

The duvet coat

How did you, how did anyone, manage before the invention of the quilted, padded duvet-style coat? It's another wonder of the modern age.

First came the duvet itself, formerly known as the

'Continental Quilt', improver of the sleep and sex lives of the British, with its flingable properties. Then came the duvet coat, enhancer of every outdoor activity from November to March.

Yes, you know about the brave Russian aristocrats who fled the Russian Revolution with nothing but their fur coat to keep them warm on their terrifying travels. That must have been a godsend. But was the fur coat, even with the family diamonds sewn into the lining, really and truly as warm as your incredible, light, puffy, machine-washable, indestructible, German-made, quilted masterpiece? It might not look as pretty as a Russian fur coat; it might have the effect of making you look like the Michelin Man, but by God, it makes you feel as snug as the Ready Brek child in an all-day body-halo of warmth.

You're trying your hardest to do your 10,000 steps a day

... and go on a special hour-long walk in the afternoon for that purpose, with a side-purpose of walking the dog. You come home, tired out after the trudge, click on the health app 'heart' to ask it, and it informs you that you've still only done 8,912 steps.

That's so mean! The standard they set is unrealistically high. You could have sworn you've done 10,000, but no, the app never lies.

Then the next day, when you're not trying at all

... just going about your ordinary life, doing two or three local errands on foot, you click on the health app at the end of the day and discover to your amazement that you've some-how, magically, done 11,702. Hallelujah! When you're least trying, you succeed.

The eerie silence of traffic-free city centres

Clop, clop, clop, clop. This is the sound of you and others at dusk on a rainy evening doing a portion of your 10,000 steps as you walk from place to place in the fifteen-minute city from which cars have been banned, or if not quite banned, then made so unwelcome by barriers, cameras, signs and fines that no one dares drive in it any more.

It should be a lovely muffled silence, in the softly falling rain: like Venice, or like a quiet suburb in the 1930s. It's some fanatical county councillor's idea of urban paradise. But actually it's a sad, echoey silence. The empty roads glisten. Occasionally an electric bike whizzes by terrify-ingly fast, leaving silence and fright in its wake, because no ear may hear it coming. The small shops can't survive on these foot customers only. Lots have closed down, so all you see is their empty, dark, stripped-out interiors through the plate-glass window, junk mail gathering dust on the carpet just inside. 'Shop To Let' boards are up. Only the charity shops, given generous rates, have a chance in this environment, so it feels like being in Prague in 1981, with musty second-hand clothes and unwanted cut-glass fruit bowls pleading for attention in shop windows.

Chips served in a silver-coloured beaker

... are a moreish delight of modern life. Poking out diagonally-vertically from inside their niftily folded cone of greaseproof paper inside the silver-coloured beaker, these chips are not so much offered as proffered. Taking one out and dipping it into whichever sauce is on offer – be it mayonnaise, hollandaise or ketchup – is an addictive pleasure. When you reach your fingers down to the tiny fallen-down offcuts at the bottom, which are really just pure deep-friedness with no potato involved, you've reached the apogee of the bliss.

In the way that beaker chips have been shaken into the cone and pre-salted, there's an echo of the McDonald's method of chip-proffering. But the beaker lifts the tone and makes the whole thing worth the restaurant price.

The list of what you're not meant to be doing or eating

... grows with every new 'health and well-being' book published during the year. Just when you most need to hunker down with a home-made moussaka, there's a radio series by a health guru telling you how to change your life in ten easy steps, and one of those steps is never to eat carbs and protein together. Another is never to drink alcohol, and another is to start the day with a cold shower.

A chocolate biscuit with your teatime cuppa? Anathema. Give it up this instant, you pathetically addicted child. The 'refined sugar' will cause a 'sugar spike' and the ensuing crash will cause havoc with your hormones and may do lasting damage to your microbiome, the recently discovered 'community' of vital bacteria living in your gut.

Basically, if you like it, crave it or enjoy it, it's bad for you. If you shudder at the thought of it, it's good for you. You're made to feel that all your own impulses are wrong, and this makes you feel somehow faulty.

And by the way, 'you need to reduce your daily eating to a six-hour window'

How could they?

The nimble-limbed author in the lacy summery dress whose book is a *Sunday Times* bestseller instructs you to choose your favoured six-hour window and stick to it. She promises you'll get used to it, and reassures you that your microbiome will thrive on it.

If you're a 'lark', she permits you to have breakfast at 12.30, and an alcohol-free healthy supper at 6 p.m. Then, nothing till noon the next day.

That sounds dismal, like the enforced diet given to someone on Death Row.

If you're a 'night owl', she instructs you to wait till 2 p.m. for your first meal of the day, but then she allows you supper at the thrillingly late hour of 7.30 p.m., as long as it's all wrapped up by 8 p.m., and then you must have nothing till 2 p.m. the next day.

Which would have a deadening effect on family life, draining it of conviviality and of what most normal people like to call 'evenings'.

Do they really expect us to live their sinisterly clean, sinless, joyless lives?

Crying at the end of the Bake Off *final*

It seems absurd, but yes, you are. The contestants are so sweet and unpretentious – and here they all are, gathered together at the picnic for extended families with the helter-skelter, and this is the final Tuesday night of all the Bake Off *Tuesday nights that have sustained you since the light evenings of September, and now the nights are drawing in, and it's all over, and the closing credits tell you that two of the contestants whom you particularly loved have since met up and 'gone on a road trip together', and that another one's gran 'passed away' in October, and this is all too much. Blinded by tears, you have to get up to grope for the box of Kleenex.*

December Screams

'If it doesn't have a screen he's not interested.'

You look at the gaping hole

… the small rectangle of blackness and nothingness, behind the '1' on the chocolate Advent calendar, whose first perforated window has been prised open and the foil film behind it ripped out with a small fingernail so the first milk chocolate bunny could be grabbed and swallowed whole.

This will be the countdown for the next twenty-four days. Window after window ripped out, contents raided, leaving a void, so by Christmas Day the shredded calendar will resemble a bombed-out block of flats in a war zone.

First Jacquie Lawson card of Advent

You're alerted to the arrival of this card in an email informing you that 'Robert and Susie has sent you a Jacquie Lawson e-card'. The Jacquie Lawson alerting system puts the verb of the sender in the singular, even if two married people have in fact sent you the card.

It instructs you to 'click on the robin to begin' – and so here you are, on 1 December, plunged deep into Christmas, with a robin flying from branch to branch, as the 'Sugar Plum Fairy' tune plays, and there's a pretty house in the snow, a blazing fire in a fireplace, a Christmas tree and a heap of wrapped-up presents, and the robin lands on a branch just outside a child's bedroom, and you want to be cynical, and it's far too early for all this, but actually you're enraptured and feel like a spoiled child and almost cry at the sweetness of it all.

The tiny black mouse droppings on the work surface

... are strangely indistinguishable from the black onion seeds inside the Gail's Potato and Rosemary Sourdough loaf.

So you're not sure whether you've 'got' mice (yet again), or whether you've just 'got' Gail's Potato and Rosemary Sourdough. Or have you perhaps got both? Does the mouse eat the black onion seed and produce an identical dropping there and then, to make up for it?

Every cultural institution you support in the whole country

... seems to be posting its annual announcement telling you they're doing a 'Big Give' this Advent, and please find it in your heart to be generous. It'll mean the world to them if you 'dig deep' and gift as much as you can. It'll help the institution to survive for another year in this 'tough climate', and will enable them to carry on with the amazing 'outreach' projects they've started doing with local primary schools.

A Big Give?

So now, not only has 'gift' become a verb, but 'give' has become a noun, like 'bake'? Instead of 'giving' a 'gift', you're being asked to 'gift' a 'give'?

How can you be singing 'O Little Town of Bethlehem'

... when it's still only 5 December? Don't they know it's only the beginning of Advent and things are supposed to carry on being subdued and full of foreboding for a bit longer yet? Surely 'the hopes and fears of all the years are met in thee tonight' should be saved up for the potentially snowy 24th?

Clearly they don't know this, as you find yourself belting out the Big Four carols – 'O Little Town', 'It Came

177

Upon the Midnight Clear', 'O Come All Ye Faithful' and 'Hark the Herald' – at the charity Christmas carol service on 5 Dec, with celebrity readers in specs who were booked for the gig back in January.

And one of celebs reads

... John Julius Norwich's *The Twelve Days of Christmas*, his witty collection of imagined thank-you letters from a young woman who receives from her admirer, first, a partridge in a pear tree, then, the next day, two turtle doves, and then, day by day, all the other twelve gifts, about which she is increasingly unenthusiastic. You heard it read aloud last year. You heard it the year before.

And another of them reads

... Carol Ann Duffy's poem about the Christmas Truce in 1914, when 'Heinrich' and 'Henry' started up a game of football in the trenches and lit Christmas lights and shook hands with each other, and it's so unbearably sad that you find yourself snuffling in the pew and have to pretend it's a bad cold, which in fact it also is.

No, thank you

No one wants a thick-lidded, non-heated-up Sainsbury's Taste the Difference mince pie with their glass of vestry-temperature white wine before supper at 7.45 p.m. on 5 Dec.

Your email suddenly stops working

You feel undone by this. All pleasure is drained out of life. How can God do this to you on a weekday evening in early December? The world needs you (at least you like to think it does). You certainly need the world. And you're cut off.

You try logging on to your emails through Google, and get lost down a vortex of password-changing confusion ('you've already registered', 'you've used this password before'), leading to the inevitable punishment of lock-out.

'If the provider of your email account supports SSL (Secure Sockets Layer) for the outgoing (SMTP) mail server, you can ask your provider to supply the information you need to connect to the outgoing mail server using SSL.'

So says your screen. Impenetrable, as usual.

You try going through the steps the screen suggests, to restore normality, but needless to say, nothing works.

Who you gonna call?

You send out the panicky WhatsApp message: 'Help! Please can you sort?'

The computer man cometh

He is today's must-have human accessory: a knight in large trainers, carrying a rucksack, who is there for you at such moments. He is today's version of Jeeves: the cool, calm, unfailingly reliable problem-solver who will schedule you in, however busy he is.

Two blue ticks! He's read your message! He's a hero already!

'Bit tied up at the mo,' he replies, 'but could poss help remotely this evening, about 7-ish?'

Or even better, 'Bit tied up at the mo, but could drop round to you guys at about 9 this evening?'

If he physically comes by, you know for certain that he will solve the problem and that you will go to sleep as a fully functioning email recipient. This knowledge is balm.

And he does come round, carrying his Chinese takeaway and can of Coke. He sits down and starts tapping away at your laptop with louder, more confident taps than you ever do. Crikey, don't break the keyboard.

But look! He's taking a while over this. Even he is not finding this an easy problem to solve. Which goes to show that you're not an idiot. Even he has to ring a call centre and be kept on hold on speakerphone for fifteen minutes while they play 'Have a Holly Jolly Christmas'.

But, after forty-five minutes at £90 an hour plus VAT, worth every penny, he gets the whole thing working and sends you an email from his phone with the word 'Test' in the subject box and no content.

It works! He's a genius.

But, upsettingly, 'Test' is the only email you receive at that moment

The world clearly didn't need you or miss you during those lost hours, it turns out.

But the next day, the Amazon emails start pinging in

... thick and fast. So at least someone is emailing you. 'Your order is confirmed.' 'Your order has been despatched.' 'Arriving today.' 'Delivered.' 'How was your delivery?'

So casual and chummy has Amazon become recently, that when you order something, it no longer makes a drama out of it. It just says, 'Order placed, thanks.' Which implies, 'Yeah, yeah, you do this every day in December, don't you, so there's no need to get excited or mention your first name each time.'

This will be the death of shops. But why go all the way to the stationery shop in the pedestrianised street to buy a large pack of coloured tissue paper when the very same item, only

cheaper, will be delivered through your letterbox tomorrow,
like a present in an easy-tear envelope?

And while you're at it, you might as well buy a box of can-
dles, 2 kg of pet food, printing ink, rinse aid, picture hooks,
scissors, chilli ketchup, vests, toothbrush heads, pens and py-
jamas, all highly available, all stored in the vast warehouse
off the M1 whose wall goes a lighter shade of blue as it reaches
the top, so it looks like the sky, but is said to be a hellhole to
work in, and you're conniving in this, but you can't resist as
it will all delivered 'by tomorrow'.

'Happy Christmas'

... 'Love, Richard and Sally.'

'PS We must get together next year!'

Well, that's a no-hoper. As you didn't manage to get
together with them this year, what makes them think it's
any more likely that you'll get together next year?

'Jason, Sue and all at J. W. Security

... wish you Happy Holidays and a great festive break!'

They flagged up Diwali, didn't they, but they now can't
bring themselves to mention Christmas, just in case it
offends and excludes.

'This toy will keep your kids away from their screens

... guaranteed!'

So says the caption under the online advertisement. And you see a flying, fluttering ball that looks like a magical item in a Quidditch game: bright blue, flying over the central island of a large open-plan kitchen. And the children are clearly loving it and are indeed not playing with their screens.

But they're children in an advertisement.

It won't keep real children away from their screens.

Well, it might, for ten minutes, from 3.10 p.m. to 3.20 p.m. on Christmas Day. But they'll be right back. Nothing keeps children away from their screens. Nothing tastes as good as screens feel.

So what on earth are you supposed to put in their stockings?

... now that they no longer read books, play with any kind of toy, look at physical maps or listen to CDs?

It'll just have to be socks, pants, T-shirts and a jar of their favourite hot sauce (hence the chilli ketchup).

183

'The puppetry is SO good!'

... you've been told, so you book expensive tickets for the sell-out show involving puppetry.

Well, the puppetry is good, except for the fact that the puppeteers are highly visible, looking like black-clad goths as they rush about in silence, manipulating the animals and the insects with their long black rods. You're not supposed to notice them, but you certainly do. You notice them so much that you fail to concentrate on the story.

The Christmas tree netter

... in the outdoor Christmas-tree pop-up shop in the park is shaped like a vast post-op cone for an extra-large hound. Buying the Christmas tree (definitely 'non-drop' this time) is made extra-specially delicious when the man emerges from his Nordic shed and feeds your chosen tree though this contraption, which spews out the correct length of white netting as the tree slowly progresses through it. Then he cuts it off with a knife in the brutal manner of a pig-castrator.

It's now easy to carry the tree home and in through the front door in this safely netted-up state.

But then you have to cut it open

... and deal with the sprawling reality of the actual tree, with its sticking-out lower branches, on which wisps of white nylon netting are still clinging like angel's hair decorations.

The Christmas turkey, stuffing and cranberry sauce sandwich

... turns out to have been a bad choice. Its chestnutty flavour does give you a shot of the imagined essence of Christmas, with the same Proustian directness as a cinamonny 'winter-scented' candle, but the soft bread sticks to the roof of your mouth, so you have to work hard with your tongue to unstick it, and then you find yourself chomping away at the hard, dried-out slices of turkey and washing it all down with a milky cappuccino and no, this is not how lunch in mid-December should be.

'It's beginning to look a lot like . . .'

Don't say it.
But the musician friend does type exactly that, finishing the sentence with the word 'Christmas' as he posts his

photo of the tree he's just put up on the beige fitted carpet in the corner of his living room next to the loudspeakers.

The useful cough

The post-pandemic lingering cough is your get-out clause for all pre-Christmas parties you don't want to go to.

'I have a hacking cough and don't want to spread my germs. Hope the party goes really well, and I'll be so sorry to miss it.' Or, 'I've got the dreaded lurgy.' And you are spared! You can crawl into bed and listen to a podcast and have a miserable, event-free, lonely life.

Or you can actually go to the party

... and have a hard time of it, as it's in a hired venue with a bar and loud music, so you can't hear a thing anyone says unless they're precisely the same height as you and speak directly into your ear. To anyone else, you have to make an agreeing, laughing expression after they've said anything, in the hope that this will 'do' as an appropriate reaction. And no one comes to top up your drink – you're meant to queue at the bar for it – and you see the occasional plate of canapés being whisked past in the distance, but they never come near you.

'It's a gift, you idiot'

… you hiss at the computer, when it asks you for 'recipient's email address'. You're making 'the recipient' a 'Friend' of the museum you love, but of course you don't want him to know about this present yet. It's meant to be a surprise for Christmas Day. But the only way to make him a 'Friend' is to do it online, and the online registering system has no concept of a gift being a surprise.

So, long before Christmas, the 'recipient' will receive the online welcome pack.

Dreading the post

It's the only time of year when you normally don't dread the post, as enough friends still do send cards with actual words in them, and the sound of them plopping onto the mat in a mini-cascade of white envelopes is delicious. Just like post used to be. And you recognise their handwriting at first glimpse: the very essence of their beloved character.

But eight days ago, you drove past a speed camera at 24 mph. And you saw the flash.

You remember the moment vividly: you were talking with the person next to you about a deep family worry. So deep was the worry that you briefly took your eye off the speedometer and went up to 24.

So now you're waiting for the brown envelope to arrive,

among the white ones. And the system that imposes this terror has no care for deep family worries being aired in cars.

'In a heavy skillet

... melt a cup of butter, add two chopped scallions ...'

What are they talking about? This is another American recipe. They speak a totally different language.

'Buy 3 for 2'

... it says, at the raw chicken breast fillets counter. You only need two packs for the recipe. But it would be crazy not to buy a third one, if it's free. So you buy three, and that's why the freezer is full of weird, whitened, ice-covered old packs of chicken breast fillets, each an extra in a long-forgotten three-for-two moment of temptation. You'll never eat those spares, because if and when you do defrost them, they come out stringy and bleached-looking, with an ancient Best Before date on them that repels.

'I'm so relieved!'

'Hugo has passed all three of his final accountancy exams. His results just came through this morning.'

Oh God. Decades after you first met this woman, when your children were at the same nursery school, here she is, still boasting about her son's successes. It used to be his flawless worksheets. Then it was his perfect GCSEs. Now it's his accountancy exams. You put a brave face on it, but this news, relayed in the park, fills you with gloom and a sense of inadequacy.

'Dear Friends and Family'

... the Christmas round robin begins, and you settle down for a fabulously amusing read. This one, from an old acquaintance who really should be forgot, begins, 'Who would have imagined a year ago that the geopolitical landscape could feel even more terrifying twelve months later. I guess we should acknowledge this before tucking in to a measure of festive jollity.'

That's her waiver, showing how politically aware she is and pre-empting the accusation that she's taking her own success too seriously, even though she is. Then this mother-of-six launches into a two-thousand-word boast about what she and the family have been doing this year, showing off her eco-virtue as she goes.

No, she and her husband didn't fly anywhere this year. They went north, not south: not to Italy, but to Shetland. North is the new south, you see, and they've been doing lots of wild swimming in lakes and the sea.

And their children are now married and/or barristers and/ or doctors.

Reading her round robin is an annual pleasure. The choicest passages are read aloud each year to guffaws.

They're dismantling the Christmas-tree shop in the park

... and it's only 20 December. Two pick-up lorries have pulled up, and there's a great whirring and clanging sound of scaffolding being unscrewed, as a team demolishes the perimeter fence, the string of lights and the Nordic shed.

But what if someone wants to put up their tree in the last few days before Christmas, as is very much the tradition in, say, Germany?

Too late, mate. Pines & Needles – or is this one called Shoots & Leaves, or is it We Tree Kings? – is being reduced to a muddy no man's land.

'Twas the night before ...'

Don't say it.

But the person you follow does type precisely those words, as she shows off her candlelit chimneypiece with four stockings hanging in a row and a glass of sherry for Father Christmas.

Midnight Mass lasts from 11.30

... till almost 1 a.m., because it's the vicar's one and only chance to entice the once-a-yearers to make churchgoing part of their lifestyle and come on ordinary non-Christmas Sundays. In order to do this, she puts her heart and soul into preaching a total Christianity-explaining, supposedly life-changing sermon, during which the once-a-yearers almost lose the will to live.

'Happy Christmas, one and all'

... posts the tipsy celebrity clergyman, back inside his vicarage after Midnight Mass, at which 'numbers were 20 per cent up on last year' and he's absolutely full of his own success, having glugged down the dregs of the communion wine.

The difference between the snowy landscape

... in the background of every Argos sale advertisement and every Christmas card you've been sent of Dutch skaters in Delft and the reality of the rainy morning outside your actual window is stark.

Today's weather has been described as 'exceptionally mild for the time of year, and wet'.

'I'm dreaming of a white Christmas.'

Well, dream on. It might be climate change or it might be sheer bad luck.

'I call this time of year "Betwixtmas"'

... posts the woman showing us her feet in snug Nordic socks as she tucks in to 'the last of the mince pies' beside her wood-burning stove.

Well, she might, but really it's 'thetimebetweenchristmasandnewyear', when everything goes blissfully quiet, except when you nip to the shops to buy a New Year present and the place is heaving. Can't these people ever stop shopping? But then you have to admit that you, too, are one of the people who can't stop shopping.

'This is not just a Wensleydale and carrot chutney sandwich'

... you read, on the packaging of the M&S sandwich you're tucking in to at the motorway service station on the way to where you're spending the New Year.

With the same enthusiasm for expanding on the noun as Kenneth Branagh showed when he said 'Freshly CAUGHT Cornish pixies' at the beginning of the second Harry Potter film, you complete the sentence in a deep, unctuous voice.

'It's an M&S Wensleydale and carrot chutney sandwich.'

It is – and in its predictable way, it's deeply comforting on this filthy afternoon when you've run in from the car and seen to your relief that there is indeed an M&S here, not just a Burger King, and you've picked out your perfect unchallenging sandwich and your craved pack of salt and vinegar crisps and have found a clean-ish table, and you suddenly feel a great outpouring of love for every single person around you, all of you basking in this moment of rest and succour on the journey.

'It's one minute to midnight!

'Quick! Switch on the TV!' And the person whose house it is does exactly that, in a bit of a panic with the remote control, and there they all are, the crowds you're delighted not to be part of, waiting for the countdown, while presenters thrust microphones in front of them.

Some people in the room are watching this on their phone. Another has switched on the radio. Two are poring over it on a laptop.

The time-lag on the various devices causes a simultaneous mass-chanting of different numbers.

'Ten!' 'Nine!' 'Four!' 'Two!' Nine!' 'Seven!' 'Eight!' 'Six!'

When does the New Year actually start?

It doesn't begin until the largest screen in the room, the television's one, homes in on beautiful, gleaming Big Ben, the epicentre of your time-telling existence.

Bong!

'Happy New Year!'

Five minutes of budget-blowing fireworks later, everyone starts slagging off the Mayor of London.

And so it rebegins.

Acknowledgements

Huge thanks to: Richard Beswick, Nithya Rae, Lucy Martin, Katy Bridgen, Marie Hrynczak and Ella Garrett at Little, Brown; Sophie Scard at United Agents; and Michael Maxtone-Smith.